Advanced Introduction to Social Policy

Elgar Advanced Introductions are stimulating and thoughtful introductions to major fields in the social sciences and law, expertly written by the world's leading scholars. Designed to be accessible yet rigorous, they offer concise and lucid surveys of the substantive and policy issues associated with discrete subject areas.

The aims of the series are two-fold: to pinpoint essential principles of a particular field, and to offer insights that stimulate critical thinking. By distilling the vast and often technical corpus of information on the subject into a concise and meaningful form, the books serve as accessible introductions for undergraduate and graduate students coming to the subject for the first time. Importantly, they also develop well-informed, nuanced critiques of the field that will challenge and extend the understanding of advanced students, scholars and policy-makers.

For a full list of titles in the series please see the back of the book. Recent titles in the series include:

Advanced Introduction to

Social Policy

DANIEL BÉLAND

Johnson Shoyama Graduate School of Public Policy, Canada

RIANNE MAHON

Balsillie School of International Affairs, Canada

Elgar Advanced Introductions

Edward Elgar
PUBLISHING

Cheltenham, UK • Northampton, MA, USA

Published by
Edward Elgar Publishing Limited
The Lypiatts
15 Lansdown Road
Cheltenham
Glos GL50 2JA
UK

Edward Elgar Publishing, Inc.
William Pratt House
9 Dewey Court
Northampton
Massachusetts 01060
USA

A catalogue record for this book
is available from the British Library

Library of Congress Control Number: 2016944275

ISBN 978 1 78347 802 6 (cased)
ISBN 978 1 78347 803 3 (paperback)
ISBN 978 1 78347 804 0 (eBook)

Typeset by Servis Filmsetting Ltd, Stockport, Cheshire
Printed on FSC approved paper
Printed and bound in Great Britain by Marston Book Services Ltd, Oxfordshire

To Angela and Rob

Contents

About the authors

Daniel Béland is Professor and the Canada Research Chair in Public Policy (Tier 1) at the Johnson Shoyama Graduate School of Public Policy, University of Saskatchewan campus. He currently serves as editor (French) of the *Canadian Journal of Sociology*, co-editor of *Global Social Policy* and President of the Research Committee 19 (Poverty, Social Welfare and Social Policy) of the International Sociological Association. A specialist of fiscal and social policy, he has published 15 books and more than 100 articles in peer-reviewed journals such as *Governance, Journal of Public Policy, Journal of Social Policy, Policy & Politics* and *Social Policy & Administration*.

Rianne Mahon holds a CIGI chair in comparative and global social policy governance at the Balsillie School of International Affairs and is a Political Science Professor at Wilfrid Laurier University. She co-edited *The OECD and Transnational Governance* (with S. McBride), *Leviathan Undone?* (with R. Keil), *Feminist Ethics and Social Politics* (with F. Robinson) and *After '08* (with S. McBride and G. Boychuk) and has written numerous articles on the place of childcare in redesigning welfare regimes at the local, national and global scales. Her current work focuses on the role of international organizations vis-à-vis the growing wave of migrant care workers.

Acknowledgements

We would like to thank the many great scholars we have collaborated with over the years, who have enriched our understanding of social policy. More specifically, we thank Rachel Hatcher for her copy-editing assistance and the two reviewers for their insightful comments and suggestions. At Edward Elgar, Commissioning Editor Emily Mew and the rest of the team did a fantastic job. It is always a pleasure to work with true professionals and we thank them for their support and assistance. Finally, Daniel Béland acknowledges support from the Canada Research Chairs Program, and Rianne Mahon from the Social Science and Humanities Council.

Introduction

In a rapidly changing world, social policy must address new social, economic, political and theoretical challenges that call into question traditional assumptions. From globalization and immigration to changing gender roles and family structures, the challenges facing contemporary social policy systems are daunting. This situation forces us to think outside the box and consider issues that social policy researchers and practitioners may have overlooked only a couple of decades ago. The field of social policy research has to adapt to a changing world, becoming increasingly aware of both global trends and enduring cross-national differences.

The objective of this *Advanced Introduction to Social Policy* is to offer a concise overview of the field that takes newer realities into account, without rejecting the insights found in the traditional social policy canon. This is why this book draws on both classic and contemporary theories and concepts to shed light on the broad processes (that is, the shift to post-industrial socio-economic structures and globalization in its multiple dimensions) that are putting pressure on existing social policy arrangements and raising new research questions. These processes in turn provide the broad canvas against which to assess the social policy implications of changing gender relations, the increasing salience of ethnic/racial/linguistic diversity among national populations and the growing importance of the Global South as a site of social policy innovation. This book also argues in favour of paying greater attention to the role of ideas in shaping social policy. Finally, it seeks to enrich comparative social policy studies by going beyond the methodological nationalism that has traditionally marked the field to include the role of transnational actors not only in shaping social policy options, but also in laying the foundations, albeit incomplete, of what could become a global social policy architecture.

While stressing the importance of contemporary challenges, the book does not ignore the forces that led to the emergence of the modern welfare state. Thus, Chapter 1 reviews the contributions of four classic thinkers—Karl Polanyi, Émile Durkheim, Richard Titmuss and T.H. Marshall—to our understanding of how social policy emerged out of the broad pressures generated by the transition to capitalist/industrial societies, while Chapter 2 provides an overview of more detailed theories that have attempted to account for why different societies have carved divergent paths to welfare state development. While these perspectives have important insights to offer even today, they are limited by their emphasis on certain actors (notably unions/parties of the left and business) over others (women, ethnic/racial/linguistic minorities), and on institutions (state structures and policy legacies), typically at the expense of ideas. They also fixed their attention primarily on Western Europe and the United States while largely ignoring the rest of the world and took the national as the key site of social policy practice for granted.

We begin to push beyond these parameters in Chapter 3. Although the chapter begins with a discussion of Gøsta Esping-Andersen's (1990, 1999) important contribution to policy studies (that is, the 'three worlds of welfare capitalism' typology), it goes beyond this to examine alternative typologies and concepts contributed by feminist theorists. In this chapter and Chapter 6, we explore the challenges posed by the ('post-industrial') shift from the male breadwinner–female caregiver to the adult earner family norm. We also examine the social forces and ideational legacies that are shaping the ways in which, and the extent to which, various societies are embracing this important transformation.

Chapter 3 also broadens the discussion to include the insights of those who have cast their sights beyond the traditional core to reflect on the variety of welfare regimes that have emerged and are emerging in the Global South. This research is important not simply because it shows that there are more than the three worlds—liberal, conservative and social democratic—Esping-Andersen identified. As the research on conditional cash transfers and social pension shows, the South has become an important site of policy innovation. Moreover, to the extent that such innovations try to grapple with the challenges created by the existence of a substantial 'informal' sector, they are also of potential interest to the North, which is facing similar problems posed by the spread of 'precarious work'.

There is also an emergent stream of research on ethnic/racial linguistic diversity and its impact not only on the development of welfare states—the classic case being the way racial divisions in the United

States contributed to the limited nature of that country's social provisions—but also on the future of welfare states even in their Western European heartland. Chapter 7 begins to take up this challenge. It builds on Fiona Williams's (1995) important insight that different conceptions of 'the nation' hold implications for whether and to what extent racialized 'others' are granted the privileges of social citizenship. It thus locates the US experience in relation to other 'white settler' societies. Some followed the US pattern but in others (Canada, New Zealand and even Sweden), social policy became one of the means for assimilating visible minorities into the dominant culture. This chapter also takes up the social policy challenges posed by the resurgence of sub-state nationalism in countries such as Belgium, Canada, Spain and the United Kingdom.

Chapter 7 also explores the issues the current wave of migration (a mix of asylum seekers, refugees and undocumented workers, largely moving from South to North) pose for existing welfare states, especially those in Western Europe. Some suggest that the very presence of such 'others' has fuelled the rise of ultra-right parties, articulating programs of 'welfare chauvinism'. Others have raised questions about the potentially corrosive impact embracing various forms of multiculturalism might have on the social solidarity required to sustain welfare states. At the same time, migrants, including 'low-skill' migrants, are in demand to meet the labour force needs of ageing Northern populations. This has led, for instance, to the creation of 'global care chains' as migrants replace the housewife-mother-daughter who once provided unpaid child and elder care work (discussed in Chapter 6).

The challenges posed to territorially-based conceptions of social rights by the increasing flow of migrants, the rediscovery of global poverty and inequality, and the social implications of climate change have helped to establish global social policy as an emerging area of research, pushing beyond the methodological nationalism of comparative social policy studies. For Deacon (2007), one of the pioneers of global social policy research, the latter has two aspects. The first involves the articulation and dissemination of social policy prescriptions by international organizations, think tanks, transnational advocacy networks and international non-governmental organizations. The second is related to the emergence of social issues that transcend national boundaries and that have given rise to the search for global solutions and a governance structure through which to pursue these. These issues are taken up in Chapter 8.

Running through the book is an emphasis on the role of ideas. Thus, in Chapter 2, we discuss theories that focus on national values as an explanation for divergent patterns of welfare state development. Contemporary students of social policy have similarly turned to the analysis of deeply embedded *cultural* assumptions to explain both political behaviour and policy development. Ideas take centre stage in Chapter 4 where we examine their role in crystallizing particular problem definitions and discuss the way ideas are used to frame social policy proposals so that these are understood as both necessary and legitimate. Policy paradigms also play a major role in the design of policy blueprints and the constructions of interests. The identification of the boundaries of policy paradigms also helps to delineate important policy shifts. Chapter 5 discusses three contemporary 'big ideas'—social exclusion, social investment and new social risks. The first two are broad policy concepts that also operate as political constructions and, as such, help shape the agenda-setting processes integral to welfare state change. The concept of new social risks is a more academic concept and, with its emphasis on the challenges posed by post-industrialism, is more akin to the broad canvass ideas discussed in Chapter 1. While we emphasize the role of ideas, it is important to remember that ideas interact with other elements. They are formulated by social agents, acting within institutional settings, which are in turn influenced by larger structural forces.

In a short book like this, it clearly was not possible to cover all contemporary social policy issues nor to discuss in great depth a number of key issues we touch upon. What the book should provide the reader is with an invitation to explore the many important issues it raises, while drawing attention to key topics that have for too long remained at the margins of mainstream social policy research.

1 Capitalism, citizenship and solidarity

The emergence of modern social programs is closely related to the advent of market capitalism and the debate over the role of the state within it (Esping-Andersen 1990). Although market capitalism brought about rapid economic development, it also generated inequalities and problems related to social cohesion. In this chapter we explore the relationship between market capitalism and social programming through a discussion of early social policy debates and scholarship. This leads to a discussion of classical social policy issues such as solidarity and social citizenship that remain central to contemporary policy debates. Reviewing the work of prominent scholars and writers from the past sheds light on broad questions central to the most current social policy research.

Market capitalism and laissez-faire

One of the best ways to grasp the relationship between market capitalism and the advent of modern social policy is to turn to the English Poor Law debate of the first half of the nineteenth century. At the time England was the epicentre of the industrial revolution and of a liberal push to extend market capitalism through free trade. In his 1944 book, *The Great Transformation*, Karl Polanyi (1944 [2001]) offered a long-term historical analysis of the English Poor Law debate that contributes to an understanding of the relationship between market capitalism and the advent of modern social policy in the nineteenth and early twentieth centuries.

The English Poor Laws had been in place since the late sixteenth century as tools of public support and social control that targeted the most vulnerable segments of the population. According to Polanyi (1944 [2001]), however, the real starting point of modern social policy was the debate over the Speenhamland Law of 1795, which resonated well beyond England and that period to shape liberal discourse about the importance of 'free markets' (or laissez-faire). The Speenhamland Law violated the then emerging liberal creed by compelling the state to offer a minimum income to the poor in the name of the 'right to live'. Under the Speenhamland Law, outdoor relief—state support granted to outside poor houses, which targeted both the unemployed and workers who received subsidies to lift their actual wages above a minimum level of income—had become widespread. Such a system, however, hindered the development of 'free labour', which was critical to the foundation of modern market capitalism. The Speenhamland Law triggered a long and intense debate that led to the passage of a dramatic Poor Law Reform in 1834, which abolished outdoor relief and the right to live.

This radical liberal reform had immediate negative social consequences. 'Many of the most needy poor', he wrote, 'were left to their fate as outdoor relief was withdrawn, and among those who suffered most bitterly were the "deserving poor" who were too proud to enter the workhouse which had become an abode of shame' (Polanyi 1944 [2001], p. 86). At the same time the 1834 reform transformed the economy in a way that facilitated the rise of modern market capitalism, based on the emergence of a competitive labour market and the 'wage society', according to which most people have to sell their labour in order to survive (Marx and Engels 1848 [1888]; Polanyi 1944 [2001]; Castel 2003). As Polanyi (1944 [2001], p. 87) put it, 'Not until 1834 was a competitive labor market established in England; hence industrial capitalism as a social system cannot be said to have existed before that date'. In England and beyond the advent of this new economic order created the need for new forms of social and labour protection. These would emerge gradually as a consequence of political struggles exacerbated by the push for free trade at the heart of mid-nineteenth century liberalism.

For Polanyi (1944 [2001], p. 144), the creation of a free labour market is only one of the three tenets of nineteenth-century liberalism. The other two are 'international free trade' and the 'automatic gold standard', where the value of a currency is tied to a certain quantity of gold. Taken together, these three elements form the utopian 'dogma of laissez-faire' that swept through Europe in the mid-nineteenth century (Polanyi 1944 [2001], p. 144). Although laissez-faire is based on the idea of spontaneous market interactions, 'There was nothing natural about laissez-faire; free markets could never have come into being merely by allowing things to take their course' (Polanyi 1944 [2001], p. 144). In fact, the triumph of laissez-faire occurred through state actions and policy decisions that imposed economic liberalism upon existing social institutions such as communal and family relations, which were badly damaged as a result. In a context of growing economic insecurity, detrimental especially to the emerging modern working class, pure laissez-faire gradually lost support as the state began to take steps to support the poor and improve the living conditions of workers and their families.

Ironically, while the imposition of laissez-faire was the product of state planning, the original reaction to the negative social consequences of unbridled market capitalism took the form of a set of spontaneous and pragmatic policy attempts to protect people and social institutions from the market. For Polanyi (1944 [2001], p. 147), 'While laissez-faire economy was the product of deliberate State action, subsequent restrictions on laissez-faire started in a spontaneous way. Laissez-faire was planned; planning was not'. Thus, the first modern social programs emerged at least in part as measures cobbled together to address social problems stemming from the imposition of laissez-faire liberalism, as the state was forced to repair the damages it had caused to the social fabric. Far from being the product of an ideological plot against laissez-faire liberalism, the gradual decline of this radical form of market capitalism in the late nineteenth and early twentieth centuries appeared as a pragmatic reaction to the social problems it had created (Polanyi 1944 [2001]).

From trade unionism to labour regulation and modern social policy, a new world emerged during these decades that witnessed the creation of the 'welfare state', a term that only became popular in the mid 1940s, at the same time as Polanyi was writing *The Great Transformation* (Béland and Petersen 2014). The consensus around the emerging welfare state proved strong across Western Europe and, after World War II, it became a central feature of modern states in Western Europe, North America and the Antipodes. Authors like Austrian economist Friedrich Hayek (2007), who condemned it in the name of personal freedom and laissez-faire, appeared as politically marginal at the time,[1] although less than three decades later Hayek's ideas would inspire a new generation of conservative politicians eager to wage an open ideological and political war on the modern welfare state.

Solidarity

Although Polanyi (1944 [2001]) might be right to point to the spontaneous nature of the early policy responses to the social problems stemming from market capitalism, many scholars and public intellectuals contributed to a critical reflection on ways to mitigate the negative impact of industrialization and market capitalism on citizens and workers. Rejecting the socialist call for a 'proletarian revolution' (an approach that triumphed in Russian in the aftermath of the 1917 October Revolution), such thinkers sketched a reformist path with which the modern welfare state gradually became associated. A striking example of this reformist stream is found in the works of French sociologist Émile Durkheim and his followers, who attempted to rethink modern solidarity as a way to move beyond purely individualistic market liberalism towards new forms of social and political integration appropriate to the industrial age.

Durkheim's 1893 book, *The Division of Labour in Society*, starts by contrasting traditional and modern societies in terms of people's economic and social interdependence (Durkheim 1893 [1997]). On the one hand, traditional societies feature a limited division of labour, which gives rise to a sense of solidarity based on sameness and the proximity of people living in the same tight-knit communities. In such a context, individuals identify spontaneously with those living around them. This type of social integration is called mechanical solidarity. In modern societies, on the other hand, a much more complex division of labour emerges according to which people performing different tasks complement one another. In contrast to Adam Smith (in his 1776 book *The Wealth of Nations* 1991) and his liberal followers, Durkheim (1893 [1997]) was not primarily interested in economic efficiency and the prosperity to which this gave rise. Instead, he was concerned with finding an appropriate model of social integration for modern societies.

For Durkheim (1893 [1997]), the division of labour is not only an economic institution but also a social form tied to a particular model of solidarity that must be nurtured to generate social integration. In contrast to the mechanical solidarity prevalent in traditional societies, in modern, capitalist societies, social integration stems from a new sense of interdependency, which he called organic solidarity. Durkheim was highly critical of what he saw as the anomic and unregulated labour relations associated with the emergent capitalist society because they contradicted the imperative of organic solidarity. As Durkheim sought to preserve the social order in modern capitalist societies, he supported the establishment of labour organizations modelled on medieval corporations so as to foster the creation of organic solidarity. Thus, although in many ways a conservative thinker, Durkheim (1893 [1997]) called for greater social solidarity, labour regulation and, to use today's language, social protection. He stopped short of advocating for the creation of state-sponsored social programs like those currently associated with the concept of the welfare state.

The most important meaning associated with the concept of solidarity then is interdependence, the recognition that people depend on one another. This idea that 'we are all in this together' is essential for understanding modern social policy debates (Béland 2010a).

In Durkheim's country, France, the intellectual movement associated with this idea and the emergence of modern social policy is *solidarisme* (Hayward 1959). As the movement's name suggests, *solidarisme* promoted greater solidarity in society as a way to address the social evils of the industrial era. Drawing on Durkheim, this movement legitimized reform in the name of greater solidarity and integration. For instance, in *Solidarité*, former politician and public intellectual Léon Bourgeois (1896 [1998]) defended a moderate reform agenda centred on the concept of solidarity found in both nature and society, which he defined as 'reciprocal dependency'. Borrowing from various sources, including biology, Bourgeois rejected market liberalism and social Darwinism and claimed that cooperation—and not competition—was the primary force in society. Criticizing excessive individualism as well as conservative hierarchies, he claimed that society is about the organic interdependency of autonomous people who need one another and society as a whole to survive and thrive as human beings. Consequently, according to Bourgeois (1896 [1998]), all people have a 'sacred debt' towards society, from which the obligations of social solidarity are derived. Such obligations include paying one's taxes and helping others in the name of human interdependency and shared social obligations.

The social reforms Bourgeois and his followers advocated included free public education, social assistance for the poor and the promotion of voluntary self-help and mutualism among workers. Later, as voluntarism proved to have limited effects, the idea of solidarity came to legitimize the development of social insurance in France (Béland and Hansen, 2000). Based on payroll contributions, social insurance is much more statist than voluntary association and self-protection, but it has proven to be a more effective tool in reducing the uncertainty facing wage workers and their families (Ewald 1986).

In France, as in many other countries, the turn to social insurance was inspired by the German model associated with Otto von Bismarck, who created the first social insurance schemes in the last decades of the nineteenth century. Bismarck's decision to create a social insurance system for blue collar workers was grounded in political calculation, as his primary goal was to weaken working class support for socialism while cementing their identification with the German state (Hennock 2007). Social insurance has, however, come to embody a form of objective solidarity, risk sharing and co-financing, which remains central to contemporary social policy research (Paugam 2011).

As Peter Baldwin (1990) suggests, however, solidarity can have potentially exclusionary occupational and class boundaries given the sometimes highly fragmented national social insurance systems that protect certain social and economic groups better than others. While some countries like Denmark and Sweden gradually extended uniform social protection to the population as a whole, others, such as Belgium and France, maintained fragmented and unequal forms of social insurance coverage that maintained and reinforced occupational boundaries of solidarity (Baldwin 1990). In other words, the development of social insurance as a form of solidarity did not always take an egalitarian form, and social policy fragmentation remains a major issue in some countries.

Occupational and fiscal welfare

According to early British social policy scholar Richard Titmuss (1958 [1963]), both occupational and fiscal welfare constitute key aspects of modern social policy. Reviewing these two issues is essential to enrich our understanding of social policy, including the issue of welfare fragmentation discussed above.

First, in his *Essays on 'The Welfare State'*, Titmuss (1958 [1963]) stresses the importance of occupational benefits granted by many employers in the context of modern industrial relations. These benefits and services can be very broad in nature, and can include 'pensions ...; death benefits; health and welfare services; personal expenses for travel; entertainment, dress and equipment; meal vouchers; motor cars and season tickets; residential accommodation; holiday expenses;

children's school fees; sickness benefits; medical expenses; education and training grants; cheap meals; unemployment benefits' and various other provisions (Titmuss 1958 [1963], pp. 50–51). Although the post-war expansion of such occupational benefits increased the welfare of a growing number of workers (and their families), Titmuss (1958 [1963]) points out that such benefits are problematic in a number of ways.

Referring explicitly to the issue of welfare fragmentation mentioned above, Titmuss (1958 [1963], p. 52) points out that these benefits have a tendency to 'divide loyalties, to nourish privilege, and to narrow the social conscience as they have already done in the United States, in France and in Western Germany'. He goes on to note that 'One fundamental question of equity that [occupational benefits] raise ... is whether and to what extent' these 'should be proportionally related to occupational and income achievement' (Titmuss 1958 [1963], pp. 52–3). As a result, occupational benefits contribute to inequalities among the workforce since some employers offer more generous and more comprehensive benefits than others. Contemporary authors have taken up the argument that private, occupational benefits raise major issues in terms of equity and inequality (Hacker 2002).

These issues are exacerbated by the fact that such unequally distributed occupational benefits are frequently subsidized by the state through tax relief (Titmuss 1958 [1963]). The costs of tax relief aimed at stimulating the development of occupational and other private benefits can be high, which is another reason why voluntary benefits are problematic. Titmuss's concerns about the use of tax instruments to influence the shape and structure of social policy are of broader relevance since such measures can encourage the development of a system offering unequal social coverage, either available through employers or by direct purchase from private insurance or financial institutions, as is the case in countries like the United States (Howard 1997).

Second, Titmuss (1958 [1963]) emphasizes the systematic relationship between taxation and social policy in his analysis of 'fiscal welfare', through which tax credits and exemptions implicitly become part of the social policy system even when they are not explicitly recognized as a form of social spending. Yet the cost of providing tax discounts for various social categories, such as parents or people taking care of dependent adult relatives, increases substantially over time. Titmuss (1958 [1963]) links this to the gradual expansion of modern income taxation, through which most 'fiscal welfare' is allocated.

In his brief historical overview of the development of 'fiscal welfare' in the United Kingdom, Titmuss (1958 [1963]) explains how the expansion of the fiscal state led to the advent of modern 'fiscal welfare' in that country. He wrote that

> [s]ince the introduction of progressive taxation in 1907 there has been a remarkable development of social policy operating through the medium of the fiscal system. This has chiefly taken the form of increasing support for the family through the recognition of more types of dependencies and substantial additions to the value of the benefits provided. (p. 45)

To illustrate this, Titmuss (1958 [1963], pp. 46–7) points to the creation of income tax child allowances, introduced in 1909 and later expanded. More generally, he argues that in the United Kingdom, the emergence of 'fiscal welfare' represented a broad transformation of the meaning of taxation, as the tax system increasingly became a tool of state-sponsored social engineering. This development suggests that social policy objectives have been progressively embedded in the tax system and that, in general, 'taxation has more or less ceased to be regarded as an impertinent intrusion into the sacred rights of private property' (Titmuss 1958 [1963], p. 46).

At the broadest level, Titmuss's analysis points to the need for social policy scholars to pay close attention to the tax system and the central role of fiscal policy within the modern welfare state, both as a source of revenues for the state and its social programs, and as a source of tax discounts for social purposes allocated to both employers and families. In other words, welfare and 'fiscal sociology' (Martin et al. 2009) are closely related and, more broadly, taxation is at the foundation of the modern state, including the welfare state (Tilly 1985). Taxation issues are especially crucial to understanding social policy in Southern Europe and the Global South, two regions of the world where tax evasion and limited state fiscal capacity are particularly central issues. However, the 'Panama Papers', leaked in early April 2016, have made it clear that the wealthy in North America and Western Europe also made use of offshore tax havens to avoid taxes in their home countries.

Social citizenship

The modern capitalist society is a fragmented class society; class inequality became a major issue across Europe during the nineteenth century, as reflected in the work of socialist thinkers like Karl Marx and Friedrich Engels (1888) and the novels of writers such as Victor Hugo, who dealt with the negative consequences of class inequality in *Les Misérables*. Thus, it is hardly surprising that the first modern social programs were explicitly associated with class. Clearly, this was the case with social assistance programs that targeted the poor in a typically punitive way, especially in the aftermath of the Poor Law reform discussed above. Social insurance, the second major type of modern social program to emerge, was explicitly associated with class in Germany, where it was first applied to the industrial working class and only later extended to other economic groups, such as farmers (Hennock 2007). From this perspective, both social assistance and social insurance programs reflected class boundaries rather than challenged them. In countries like Denmark and Sweden, however, more inclusive social programs grounded in cross-class political alliances emerged to lay the foundations for what would become a universal welfare state. The latter aimed to build a form of social solidarity that transcended social classes by bringing all citizens together under the same basic social policy system (Baldwin 1990). The rise of universality, which triumphed in the United Kingdom as well as Scandinavia after 1945, is closely associated with the idea of social citizenship captured in the work of British sociologist T.H. Marshall.

In 'Citizenship and social class', Marshall (1964) reflected on long-term historical changes that culminated in the late 1940s with the creation of universal social programs such as the National Health Service (NHS) under the Labour government of Clement Atlee (1945–51). Given that it provided access to health care on the basis of citizenship rather than need (social assistance) or past contributions (social insurance), the NHS belonged to a third—universal—type of social program. Today, universal programs remain a major type of social policy, alongside social assistance and social insurance (Béland 2010a).

The advent of universal welfare in post-war Britain stems partly from the war effort and the sense of national solidarity it created (Titmuss 1958 [1963]). This sense of national solidarity and shared citizenship was reflected in an important report written by William Beveridge (1942), which advocated the introduction of comprehensive social policy reform after the war. This widely circulated report did much to legitimize the extension of social policy coverage after 1945, not only in the United Kingdom but also elsewhere in Europe and beyond, especially in Commonwealth countries such as Canada (Rice and Prince 2013, p. 63).

Marked by the optimism of the early post-war era, in his classic essay Marshall (1964) tells of the linear extension of modern citizenship that emerged in response to the tension between social inequality and the imperative of 'basic human equality' derived from one's 'full membership' in a political community. For Marshall (1964), the most fundamental issue at stake was the contradiction between the existence of capitalist class inequality and the need for recognizing each individual as a full member of the political community. Like others, Marshall's (1964) analysis portrayed modern citizenship as the extension of social protection and redistribution through the recognition and differentiation of rights by the modern national state.[2]

For Marshall (1964), modern citizenship can be understood in terms of three categories of rights—civil, political and social—that, he argues, emerged chronologically. Civil rights represent the foundation of modern citizenship, but also the ground from which capitalism grows. Indeed, what he calls civil citizenship 'is composed of the rights necessary for individual freedom—liberty of the person, freedom of speech, thought and faith, the right to own property and to conclude valid contracts, and the right to justice' (Marshall 1964, p. 71). Emerging during the eighteenth century, the idea of economic freedom was accepted as idiomatic by the beginning of the following century, notably with the repeal of the Elizabethan statutes (Marshall 1964, p. 76). The generalization of civil rights—at the centre of the liberal crusade—leads to the establishment of a 'market society' (Polanyi 1944 [2001]). The protection of individual rights, such as private property, stimulates the emergence of a new system of economic regulation where the state is expected to perform only a small number of basic tasks, such as policing and military protection. According to Marshall (1964), modern social classes are the product of this capitalist system, a system that could not exist without the protection of individual freedom and property rights.

The history of the second category of rights 'is different both in time and in character' (Marshall 1964, p. 77). Emerging after the recognition/protection of most civil rights, political citizenship is not about the creation of new rights but 'the granting of old rights to new sections of the population' (Marshall 1964, p. 77) through the gradual recognition of universal suffrage. When women gained the right to vote, the basis of political rights shifted 'from economic substance to personal status' (Marshall 1964, p. 78). As political rights became an integral part of egalitarian citizenship, private property and class position were no longer the formal basis of political participation. If civil rights constituted the liberal component of modern citizenship, then the enlargement of political rights created a democratic order that gradually extended political participation.

For Marshall, the recognition of social rights was a response to the tensions between capitalist class inequality and the imperative of equality derived from full political membership. Through the development of benefits and social services, the state protects individuals against economic risks, such as unemployment, while reducing the scope of inequality in the capitalist society. As he states,

> [t]here is a general enrichment of the concrete substance of civilized life, a general reduction of risk and insecurity, an equalization between the more and the less fortunate at all levels—between the healthy and the sick, the employed and the unemployed, the old and the active, the bachelor and the father of a large family. Equalization is not so much between classes as between individuals within a population which is now treated for this purpose as though it were one class. Equality of status is more important than equality of income. (Marshall 1964, p. 102)

To summarize Marshall's argument, social citizenship represents both the extension and the transformation of a liberal logic of protection. It is aimed at reducing the level of insecurity and inequality created by the capitalist system.

Perhaps the most obvious problem with Marshall's analysis of modern citizenship is that it does not place sufficient emphasis on the political struggles and the bargaining processes that could explain 'where rights come from' (Tilly 1998). For example, references to gender inequality are rare in 'Citizenship and social class', an essay in which 'the *male* worker serves as the ideal-typical citizens' (Orloff 1993a, p. 308). Another problem with Marshall's genealogy of citizenship is that it is overly linear, not to mention UK-centric, which means that it lacks comparative depth (Bulmer and Reeds 1996).

Conclusion

The early scholarship on social policy discussed in this chapter allowed us to take a broad look at key issues such as market liberalism, solidarity, social citizenship and fiscal welfare that remain central to contemporary social policy debates. From our perspective, however, the issues this early scholarship excluded also point to the blind spots of early social policy research, many of which are addressed in the rest of this book. First, the early scholarship largely remained silent about gender. Second, this scholarship had little to say about issues such as immigration, ethnicity and 'race'. Third, this scholarship took the spatial and territorial organization of welfare—its centralization at the national scale—for granted, while neglecting issues such as decentralization and federalism, which have long been crucial in many countries. Finally, with the partial exception of the work of Titmuss (1958 [1963]), the early scholarship devotes only limited attention to rigorous, systematic and historically informed comparative analysis aimed at explaining differences among countries in terms of social provision. This flaw is explicitly addressed in more recent welfare state development literature reviewed in the next chapter.

NOTES

1 The situation was different in the United States. In that country, although state interventionism triggered by the New Deal and World War II remained strong, the term 'welfare state' came under attack after 1945 (Béland and Petersen 2014).

2 The following paragraphs are adapted from Béland (2005a).

2 Explaining social policy development—theoretical perspectives

In recent decades, much has been written about the economic, social and political conditions associated with the emergence of modern welfare states. The goal of these works is not only to account for the advent of modern social programs but also to explain variation in the level and nature of social provision offered within each jurisdiction. In this chapter we evaluate these theories in light of their capacity to explain the abundant cross-national differences in welfare provision. One of the classic questions is why public social programs are so much less developed in the United States than in most Western European countries. Also, how have Nordic countries like Sweden been able to build such comprehensive social protection systems based on the principle of universality? It is only by keeping such questions in mind that we can adequately assess the respective contributions of the main theories of welfare state development—industrialism, national values, power resource, business power, and historical institutionalism (Myles and Quadagno 2002; Skocpol 1992; Béland 2010a).

Industrialism

One important focus of the literature related to the development of the welfare state focuses on the impact of industrialization and related social and economic forces on the advent of modern social programs. Originally formulated by authors such as Clark Kerr and his colleagues (1960), this literature is based on the assumption that 'Industrialization creates new demands for public spending as systems of social support based on kinship and the patrimonial traditions of agrarian societies are eroded' (Myles and Quadagno 2002, p. 36). In other words, modern economic development, which, as Durkheim reminded us (Chapter 1), weakens traditional families and communities, creates a new need for state intervention. This approach focuses less on the negative impact of laissez-faire as Polanyi (1944 [2001]) did than on the demographic and social consequences of industrialization that make state intervention increasingly necessary (Wilensky and Lebeaux 1958; Rimlinger 1971; Wilensky 1975). Industrialism can thus be seen as a structural approach (Parsons 2007) to welfare state development as it depicts economic change as the prime mover of social and political change.

Harold Wilensky (1975) is one of the most influential scholars working in this tradition. While building on other theories of welfare state development, Wilensky brought quantitative methods to bear on the subject (Myles and Quadagno 2002, p. 36). Wilensky (1975, p. xiii) summarizes the findings of his seminal book, *The Welfare State and Equality*, as follows:

> On the basis of a cross-sectional analysis of sixty-four countries, I conclude that economic growth and its bureaucratic and demographic outcomes are the root cause of the general emergence of the welfare state—the establishment of similar programs of social security, the increasing fraction of GNP [gross national product] devoted to such programs, the trend toward comprehensive coverage and similar methods of financing.

Yet, when he attempts to explain cross-country differences in social provision, Wilensky moves away from a strictly structural perspective. For Wilensky (1975, p. xiv), it is 'specific differences in political, social, and economic organization' that explain why 'rich countries diverge' in terms of the scope of social provision they offer. Such differences include 'the degree of centralization of government, the shape of the stratification order and related mobility rates, the organization of the working class, and the position of the military' (Wilensky (1975, p. xiv).

This last quote is important for two reasons. First, it suggests that economic factors such as industrialization cannot alone account for cross-country variation. In other words, as a theory of welfare state development, industrialism is incomplete. Although structural changes matter for welfare state development, countries with similar levels of economic and industrial development can end up with very different social policy systems. We need only to think of the marked differences between the social policy systems of the United States and a number of European countries with similar levels of economic development (Skocpol 1992). Second, to explain cross-national differences in social provision, scholars frequently have to combine different elements drawing on different theoretical perspectives (Myles and Quadagno 2002), as is often the case in doing social science analysis because one approach alone is often unable to explain particular outcomes (Parsons 2007).

These two remarks need to be kept in mind as we review other perspectives on welfare state development. Theoretical labels are useful for identifying various explanatory factors, but to solve particular empirical puzzles about welfare state development, it is often necessary to have recourse to different theoretical approaches. In other words, theoretical labels are only there to clarify distinctions between different types of explanation. They should not be used to create artificial boundaries between scholars based on their primary analytical perspectives.

National values

The next approach is associated with the work of authors such as David Levine (1988) and Seymour Martin Lipset (1990). It is rooted in the assumption that cross-national variation in cultural values (taken for granted assumptions about the social and economic world) accounts for differences in welfare state development among advanced industrial countries. This approach suggests that broad, widely shared cultural beliefs shape the mind of voters and policy makers, leading them to select particular policy options rather than others (Levine, 1988). From a methodological standpoint, this simply means that the scope and structure of national social policy systems reflect differences in cultural values typically measured through public opinion data.

A classic example of this approach is Lipset's (1990) *Continental Divide.* Lipset claims that social programming is less comprehensive in the United States than in Canada because of historically constructed differences in national values that are readily apparent in public opinion and survey data. Although these two countries have a lot in common compared to their European counterparts, the push for welfare state development has been weaker in the United States due to the greater prevalence of individualistic values there than in Canada. As he notes, 'In comparison to Great Britain and much of Europe, Canada and the United States share the same values, but in Canada they are held more tentatively. Canada's closer links to its European origins have helped perpetuate elements of an older set of beliefs.' For Lipset (1990: 4), the beliefs associated with the statist tradition of Toryism inherited from Britain and the presence of 'more state-related and less-individualistic and moralistic church traditions' in Canada than in the United States account for the former's more comprehensive and universalistic social program development than in the latter. The problem with this approach, as with that focused on industrialism, is its high level of generality. This prevents these theories from accounting for sometimes profound internal variation in welfare state development across policy areas within the same country (Skocpol 1992; Béland 2010a). More rigorous comparison of social policy in Canada and the United States makes it clear that each social policy area is distinct and that the differences and similarities between these two countries vary from one area to the next. For example, both the Canadian and the US pension systems rely extensively on private benefits, but this is not the case with their respective health care sectors (Béland and Gran 2008). There the contrast between the universality of Canadian health care and incomplete private coverage for the working population in the United States remains striking, even after the signing of the Affordable Care Act in 2010.

To account for such complex national and cross-national patterns by referring to broad national values is potentially misleading. A more detailed institutional and political analysis, attentive to the forces driving policy design in each policy area, is required (Skocpol 1992; Myles 1998). The ideational perspective formulated in Chapter 4 takes these critical remarks into account to move the study of culture and social policy forward.

Power resource

Power resource theory was developed as an alternative to functionalist explanations of welfare state development, such as those discussed above. While various authors have contributed to this tradition,[1] it is most closely associated with the pioneering work of Walter Korpi (1978, 1980, 1983) and, later, Gøsta Esping-Andersen (1985a).

Stimulated in part by the revival of Marxist thinking,[2] Korpi was nonetheless critical of Marxist conceptions of power. He agreed with Marxists that the main power resources in society are those of the 'fundamental' classes, that is, the bourgeoisie, whose power derives from its control over the means of production, and the working class, whose power derives from the development of organizations—mainly unions and parties of the left—capable of organizing workers as a class. The strength of the working class could thus be measured in terms of the proportion of the labour force that is unionized and the proportion of the electorate supporting parties of the left. Unlike Marxists, however, Korpi (1980, p. 309) believed in the potential for workers to use their power resources to shape public policies in such a way as to significantly reduce inequality:

> Where the working class has been strongly mobilized and has achieved a relatively stable control over the government, a crucial decrease in the difference between the power resources of the main classes in capitalist democracies has occurred. This ... improves the relative position of the still weaker working class and opens up new alternatives for action for this class ... [making] it possible for the working class to use public policy to intervene in the distributive processes in society.

As the above quotation suggests, the welfare state constitutes a particularly important stake in this conflict.

For Korpi (1980), it is not simply a question of 'how much' a state comes to spend on social policies or even how much a state intervenes in the labour market by setting minimum wages or establishing legislation favourable to unions. What is of particular importance is the form that social expenditure takes. Here Korpi (1980), as with Esping-Andersen (1985a, 1985b, 1990) after him, was influenced by Titmuss's distinction between residual, occupational and institutional patterns, discussed in Chapter 1. For Korpi (1980) and Esping-Andersen (1985a, 1985b, 1990), the institutional form is the most likely to increase workers' power resources. In contrast to residual policies that separate the poor from the rest by including better off parts of the working class, programs built along institutional lines establish a promising basis for coalitions uniting all workers and the middle class.

Esping-Andersen (1985a, 1985b, 1990) built on the foundations Korpi (1980) had laid. He agreed that unions and parties of the left constituted important power resources but argued that 'the effectiveness of working class power resources depends on: the extent to which the non-socialist parties are initially divided; and the conditions open to working class parties to forge alliances with other social classes' (1985b, p. 223). The first point is simple enough: if a left-leaning party, strongly backed by an effective union movement, faces a divided opposition, it will be easier for it to gain office and begin to implement its program. It also makes it more likely that it will be in office long enough to embed its social policies firmly.

Esping-Andersen's second point, however, is an important addition to Korpi's (1980) framework. Esping-Andersen (1985b, p. 224) recognized that 'a majority based solely on traditional working class votes is unlikely to occur and equally unlikely to be stable'. In the context of the transition to full-fledged capitalism, the most likely allies for workers were to be found in the rural sector, especially where the latter was primarily organized on 'family farms', as opposed to large estates reliant on peasant labour under the dominion of the landlord. Social democratic arguments for basic universal policies constitute a basis for forging such an alliance with farmers. However, once the shift to capitalism has succeeded in reducing the relative amount of the rural population, the new middle class of employees constitutes the most important potential ally for the working class. The middle class, however, requires more than flat-rate universal programs, as these are insufficient for them to maintain their lifestyles in case of unemployment, sickness or retirement. To prevent the middle class from opting out, as well as to ensure high quality public services, it is therefore important to introduce the principle of income replacement into public social insurance programs.

The focus on (variable) power resources would later lead Esping-Andersen (1990) to develop a system for classifying welfare states. Before we discuss this, however, it is important to consider two other theoretical approaches. One can be seen as a counter to Korpi and Esping-Andersen's emphasis on working class power in that it draws attention to the role played by business. The other can be seen as a wider theoretical framework that can easily encompass Esping-Andersen's work.

Business power

While many social policy scholars have followed power resource theorists' focus on variations in working class power, others have stressed the impact of business on social programming. Perhaps because employers play such a direct role in US (private) social provision, these approaches have been especially influential in the United States, where scholars have tried to explain the particular trajectory of their country's social policy development.

One influential theory of welfare state development in the United States is the corporate liberalism model. Starting from the assumption that labour power is particularly weak in the United States, proponents of this approach, such as Colin Gordon (1991), Jill Quadagno (1984) and William Domhoff (1996), stress the direct influence of progressive industrialists on the formulation of major social policy legislation. According to Domhoff (1996), for instance, the interests of a particular, reformist faction of the capitalist class shaped the content of the 1935 Social Security Act (SSA), which introduced the first federal social insurance program in the United States. From this perspective, the fact that employers played such a direct role in the formulation of social programs explains why market-friendly policies have proved so dominant. The corporate liberalism model has been criticized for neglecting the role of other powerful actors, such as state bureaucrats, in policy making and for offering a simplistic analysis of the policy process that amounts 'to little more than documenting a personal contact between a capitalist and a legislator or an executive official' (Skocpol 1992, p. 27).[3]

A more sophisticated understanding of the potential impact of business power in welfare state development has emerged from the debate between Peter Swenson (1997) and Jacob Hacker and Paul Pierson (2002). On the one hand, Swenson (1997) argues that the 1935 SSA was designed to accommodate and co-opt business interests, a situation made clear by the fact that business opposition to the SSA rapidly faded after its enactment. On the other hand, Hacker and Pierson (2002) claim that policy decisions can shape business interests. Thus, in 1935 and after, business interests simply adapted to the Roosevelt administration's social policies. At the same time, they acknowledge the impact of business power at the state level. More broadly, Hacker and Pierson (2002) highlight the way that political institutions such as federalism filter the political impact of business interests. Once again, one theoretical perspective (business power) is combined with another (historical institutionalism, which is reviewed below).

Finally, it is difficult to discuss the role of employers in the development of social programs without mentioning the 'varieties of capitalism' school, which 'highlights the importance of social policy to firms and the role that business groups play in the development of welfare states' (Hall and Soskice 2001, p. 50). In fact, this approach combines functionalist and institutionalist assumptions to the extent that it posits 'there should be a correspondence between types of political economies and types of welfare states' (Hall and Soskice 2001, p. 50). Accordingly, this approach identifies two main types of political

economies in the advanced industrial world: liberal market economies, such as Australia, Canada, the United Kingdom and the United
States, and coordinated market economies, such as France, Germany,
Japan and Sweden (Hall and Soskice 2001). Drawing on the same
approach, Isabela Mares (2003) stresses the central role of business
interests in welfare state development across the advanced industrial
world.

Korpi (2006) responded both to historians like Swenson and to varieties of capitalism scholars by arguing that, in analysing the politics of
welfare development, it is important to distinguish between protagonists, antagonists and consenters. For Korpi, business is rarely a protagonist, though, as in the example of Roosevelt's New Deal, it can play
the role of consenter. This distinction among the three roles would
later be picked up by others to produce an insightful synthesis of power
resource and varieties of capitalism (see Chapter 6).

Historical institutionalism

Along with power resource theory, historical institutionalism is perhaps the most influential approach to understanding welfare state
development. Several of the scholars cited above, most notably Hacker
and Pierson (2002), highlight the role of political institutions and policy
legacies in welfare state development. Historical institutionalism is a
broad perspective that is easily combined with other approaches. It is
not only used to analyse social policy development but also applies to
a variety of research areas (Steinmo et al. 1992; Weaver and Rockman
1993; Immergut 1998). Nevertheless, influential welfare state scholars,
such as Skocpol (1992), Ann Orloff (1993b) and Paul Pierson (1993)
clearly locate their work in relation to this tradition.

Historical institutionalism finds its origin in state-centred approaches
that advocated 'bringing the state back in' in reaction to society-
centred approaches that focused on economic factors (industrialism)
and social classes (power resource theory) and, as a result, tended to
marginalize the role of the state (Evans et al. 1985). For Skocpol (1985,
p. 9), one of the founders of historical institutionalism, the state needs
to be treated as an autonomous factor because

> States conceived as organizations claiming control over territories and
> people may formulate and pursue goals that are not simply reflective of the

demands or interest of social groups, classes, or society. This is what is usually meant by 'state autonomy'. Unless such independent goal formulation occurs, there is little need to talk about states as important actors.

Once the relative autonomy of the state from societal actors is recognized, as Skocpol (1985, p. 9) claims, scholars need to 'explore the "capacities" of states to implement official goals, especially over the actual or potential opposition of powerful social groups or in the face of recalcitrant socio-economic circumstances'.

Skocpol's thesis that the state does not merely reflect the material interests of business and labour organizations was the starting point of historical institutionalism, which moved rapidly away from a focus on state autonomy to formulate a more complex understanding of the ways in which political institutions and existing policy legacies shape the mobilization of interest groups and other social actors in general and of welfare state development in particular. This approach is clearly formulated in Skocpol's (1992) seminal book, *Protecting Soldiers and Mothers*, which attempts to explain why the United States took a different path to welfare state development than its European counterparts. For Skocpol (1992), political institutions such as party systems and constitutional design (degree of power centralization and state capacity) filter the mobilization of social and economic actors. Simultaneously, existing policies create institutional constraints and opportunities for reformers, who rarely start from *tabula rasa*. Rather, they must take into account existing social programs in attempting to bring about policy change.

With regard to political institutions, variation in electoral rules and party systems can have an impact on welfare state politics, as some systems may diffuse power while others tend to concentrate it. The contrast between the decentralized United States and the centralized United Kingdom (at least until the wave of devolution in the late 1990s) illustrates this point. Due to the division of power between the president and the two houses of Congress and the absence of party discipline in Congress, federal power in the United States is fragmented. This is in marked contrast to the situation prevailing in Westminster, where party discipline and the fusion of executive and legislative powers associated with the cabinet structure tend to concentrate political power, at least when a majority government is in power. As Paul Pierson (1994) suggests, however, the institutional concentration of power is not always a good thing for politicians, at least when they try to diffuse blame stemming from potentially unpopular measures such as tax increases or benefit cuts. In other words, the role of formal political institutions is complex and multifaceted, and their impact varies depending on the context.

For example, the impact of federalism on the welfare state varies substantially from country to country, and even from policy area to policy area within the same country (Obinger et al. 2005). Although federalism and decentralization may hinder welfare state expansion, under some circumstances they can help bring about such expansion. This is what occurred in post-World War II Canada, where state-building competition between the federal government and the provinces led to a gradual expansion of social programming and the creation of a universal health care system in the mid to late 1960s. According to Antonia Maioni (1998), this situation also reflected the impact of third parties on the left of the political spectrum, who pressured the federal state (especially in times of minority government) to expand social programs. These parties did not exist in the United States, a country where, on average, federalism had a more negative impact on social policy development (Maioni 1998).

Concerning policy legacies, historical institutionalism is grounded in the assumption that existing social policies shape the politics of reform through what is known as policy feedback, a concept that refers to how policies affect politics over time (Pierson 1993; Béland 2010b). For example, policies enacted decades ago have since created bureaucratic constituencies and large numbers of beneficiaries who have a large stake in the future of the social programs they rely on (Pierson 1993). From a historical institutionalist standpoint, this results in the resilience of social policy institutions over time, as they create constraints and opportunities for future reformers. Yet, as R. Kent Weaver (2010) has argued, feedback effects stemming from existing social programs are not always self-reinforcing, as economic and demographic factors may gradually exacerbate their inner institutional vulnerabilities. Thus, in contrast to Pierson's (1993) argument, policy feedback does not always lead to institutional continuity and path dependence (that is, a strong, self-reinforcing form of policy continuity) (Weaver 2010).

Conclusion

Each of the traditional theories reviewed has a contribution to make in understanding welfare state development because each emphasizes certain factors that can shape welfare state development depending on the context and the policy area concerned. Explanations of cross-national differences in social policy need to consider all these dimensions. Rather than trying to find a grand theory that can explain all such differences, an inductive, empirically grounded approach is more rewarding.

In fact, scholars engaged in rigorous studies of welfare states frequently draw insights from several theoretical perspectives simultaneously. For instance, in *Development and Crisis of the Welfare State*, Evelyne Huber and John D. Stephens (2001) combine insights from historical institutionalism and power resource theory in a coherent and systematic manner. This is hardly surprising because power resource scholars like Esping-Andersen (1990) put institutional logics at the centre of their analysis. As we shall see in Chapter 3, Esping-Andersen's work on welfare regimes overlaps with historical institutionalism (Esping-Andersen 1990). This suggests that, although helpful, the typology of theories discussed in this chapter should not obscure the analytical overlaps that arise in the work of many scholars.

Combining insight from different approaches is perfectly legitimate for social policy researchers as long as they properly define the different explanatory factors they identify, draw a clear line among them and explain how they combine these factors to account for particular empirical puzzles (Parsons 2007). Theories of welfare state development should be taken seriously in their own right but they are not always mutually exclusive and, more importantly, they can be combined, as long as this is done rigorously.

NOTES

1 See, for example Martin (1975) and Stephens (1979).

2 For two examples of neo-Marxist work on the welfare state, see O'Connor (1973) and Gough (1979).

3 In some respects this is an unfair criticism of the revisionist historians. For instance, G.W. Domhoff (1970) focused on the critical role played by think tanks associated with different fractions of American capital.

3 Classifying countries— reconsidering welfare regimes

More than 15 years after the publication of *The Three Worlds of Welfare Capitalism*, Esping-Andersen's (1990) three worlds thesis remains central to debates about how to classify and thus to compare welfare states.[1] His main contributions include the concept of 'welfare regime', which focuses attention on the distinct organizational logics that underlie a range of social policies, and the related concepts of decommodification and stratification used to differentiate regimes. The concept of regime also calls attention to the complex relationship between politics and policy such that, while politics initially shapes social policy regimes, the latter in turn have an impact on subsequent political alignments. In this respect, his analysis has much in common with historical institutionalist theories discussed in Chapter 2, including the shared assumption of path-dependent responses to contemporary challenges.

Of course, this does not mean that the theses laid out in *Three Worlds* and in *Social Foundations of Postindustrial Economies* (1999) have gone uncontested. They were and continue to be challenged along a variety of lines. As we shall see, some have argued that closer comparative analysis of social policies in Organisation for Economic Co-operation and Development (OECD) countries reveals more than three worlds of welfare capitalism, while others would highlight intra-regime differences. The main challenges, however, have come from feminists, who have argued the need to 'gender' welfare regimes with great effect, and from those who look beyond the Global North to explore welfare regimes in various parts of the South, as well as in the former Soviet bloc. Bringing gender in makes visible the various ways in which women are treated unequally in the labour market and by the state and highlights their (often unpaid) contribution to social reproduction. Although perhaps 25 years ago, Esping-Andersen and others writing on welfare states could afford to limit their attention to Western Europe, North America and the Antipodes, such selectivity is no longer valid in the twenty-first century when important social policy innovations are being undertaken in Latin America, Asia and Africa.

The first section of this chapter examines Esping-Andersen's conception of welfare regimes, tracing its roots to the classics explored in the previous two chapters. The second section discusses feminist contributions to welfare regime theory, including the (partial) impact their work has had on mainstream comparative approaches. The third section turns to the contributions of those who examine the worlds of social provision largely ignored by Esping-Andersen and other Northern scholars.

Three worlds of welfare capitalism

Esping-Andersen was by no means the first to notice that social policy patterns differed cross-nationally. As early as the 1950s, Wilensky and Lebeaux (1958, p. 138) contrasted countries where a 'residual' approach, which limits state involvement to cases where markets and families fail, predominated to those where social policies operate as 'first line functions' of society. However, they believed that pressures associated with industrialization would lead to convergence towards the institutionalist approach. Esping-Andersen (1990) made no such assumption. Rather, looking at social policy patterns that had been established by the 1980s in 18 OECD countries, he highlighted the persistence of three different patterns: a liberal regime, where means-tested social assistance is supplemented by modest universal transfers or similarly modest social insurance programs, leaving the rest to markets and/or families; a corporatist regime, where segmented social insurance programs predominate and 'the state will only interfere when the family's capacity to service its members is exhausted' (1990, p. 27); and a social democratic regime, based on high quality universal programs, which also 'preemptively socialize the costs of familyhood' (1990, p. 28). The United States best exemplifies the first, although Australia, Canada, the United Kingdom, Ireland and New Zealand were also classified as liberal. Germany best exemplifies the corporatist pattern, also found in the other continental West European countries. Sweden and Norway best exemplify the social democratic pattern, although the latter can also be found in Denmark and to a lesser extent in Finland.

In broad outline, these three worlds build on Titmuss's (1974) distinction between residual, industrial achievement-performance and institutional-redistributive patterns. What Esping-Andersen (1990) added were the concepts of stratification and decommodification. The first concept, touched on in Chapter 1, is fairly straightforward. It is clear that the liberal regime, with its recourse to stigmatizing means-tested assistance, marks the poor out from the rest, while corporatist social insurance schemes offer distinct programs for different class and status groups and social democratic regimes, with their emphasis on universal social programs of high quality, are encompassing. The concept of decommodification, drawn from Marshall's (1964) and Polanyi's (1944 [2001]) work discussed in Chapter 1, is more complex. Marshall's reflections on social citizenship raised the possibility that social policies could lead to the attenuation of class inequality. Polanyi put the issue more sharply: as laissez-faire capitalism treated labour as a mere commodity, social policies were needed to curtail the power of the market, thereby re-embedding labour in society. From this Esping-Andersen (1990, p. 22) derived his concept of decommodification, which occurs 'when a service is rendered as a matter of right, and when a person can maintain a livelihood without reliance on the market'. We shall look at feminist and other critiques below; here it is important to clarify what Esping-Andersen meant.

At first glance, decommodification seems to point to a socialist, rather than a social democratic, utopia, but Esping-Andersen (1990, p. 23) qualified his definition in two ways. First, decommodifying social policies include social insurance programs that guarantee benefits are equal to normal earnings and are of sufficient duration. In contrast, liberal regimes, both those that rely on means-testing and meagre benefits and those that simply offer universal, flat-rate benefits, do the least to decommodify. While corporatist regimes offer more generous benefits, these are contingent on work-related contributions. Second, Esping-Andersen did not mean that people could simply avoid work. For him, full employment constitutes a key component of a social democratic regime: it attenuates the power of capital (as Kalecki 1942 [1972] observed), and it is necessary if the state is to have the revenue needed to support a decommodifying welfare regime.

Esping-Andersen (1990) sought an explanation for the existence—and persistence—of these three regimes in a version of the power resource theory discussed in Chapter 2. He highlighted the following three aspects: 'the nature of class mobilization (especially of the working class); class-political coalition structures; and the historical legacy of regime institutionalization' (1990, p. 29). Thus, where strong unions and parties of the left have helped to develop workers' identification as members of a class with interests of its own, but one that can also forge effective coalitions with others—initially small farmers and subsequently wage earners of the new middle class—social democratic welfare regimes are most likely to emerge. By offering universal benefits of high quality, such regimes foster broad cross-class commitment to the welfare state. In contrast, when unions focus on sectional interests and/or espouse business-unionism and left-leaning parties are relatively weak, liberal welfare regimes are most likely to predominate. Limited support for the new middle class then fosters the expansion of market-based insurance and other private measures that undercut demand for universal programs. The relative importance of states and markets in social provision constitutes an important dividing line between welfare regimes. This is especially visible in areas such as health care and pensions, where some countries like the United States subsidize private benefits and services in a regressive way, from both a fiscal and a social standpoint (Hacker 2004; Howard 2006; Béland and Gran 2008).

Finally, corporatist arrangements emerged where the working class was relatively isolated, initially by the predominance of a rural sector divided between landed aristocracies and a peasantry. Stratified social insurance programs built along Bismarckian lines were instituted as a way of pre-empting working class mobilization. This established a social policy structure that fostered loyalty to status-segregated programs on the part of the emerging middle classes. The strength of religion-based parties (Christian Democrats) also helped reinforce the concept of subsidiarity (that is, reliance on the family), while the structure of family benefits encouraged mothers to stay at home (Esping-Anderson 1990, p. 27).

A final contribution of Esping-Andersen's (1990) three worlds is his thesis that the type of welfare regime affects a country's post-industrial trajectory. Taking the United States, Germany and Sweden as his examples, Esping-Andersen argued that the US liberal regime has created some good, but also many poorly paid service sector jobs, with many of the latter in the food, cleaning and lodging services. In contrast, the Swedish social democratic regime, with its strong social service sector, has created numerous good and middle-level service sector jobs, while the German post-industrial structure is concentrated at the top and is less developed (1990, p. 206).

We shall examine the main criticisms of the three worlds in the next sections. Here, however, it is worth considering those who contested his initial typology.[2] Some have argued that Southern Europe (Ferrera 1996) or the 'Latin Rim' (Leibfried 1992) constitute a fourth regime. Ferrera's argument is the most elaborated. For him, the Southern European model deviates significantly from the corporatist version in the northern part of the continent in that its system of social insurance is highly fragmented, marked by 'peaks of generosity and . . . macroscopic gaps in provision'; the establishment of a universal health care system; a low degree of state penetration of welfare leaving an important role for non-public actors; and the persistence of clientelism (Ferrera 1996, pp. 29–30). Clientelism results from weak state institutions, especially the bureaucracy and the prominence of parties as instruments of patronage distribution. There is also a significant informal sector in these countries, a point that Ferrera notes but does not highlight (1996, p. 32). As we shall see, clientelism and the existence of a significant informal sector are elements that this model has in common with some of the patterns found in the Global South.[3]

Castles and Mitchell (1993, p. 105) argued for a different 'radical'—in terms of its 'equalizing potential'—world largely made up of Anglophone countries (that is, Australia, New Zealand, Britain, Ireland and Canada). The latter's profile of low expenditure, high equalizing instruments is said to reflect the presence of 'a strong labour movement [that] has found it difficult to translate popular support into cabinet incumbency during the post-war era' (Castles and Mitchell 1993, p. 119). Castles and Mitchell (1993) also note the similarity between the antecedents of the radical Anglophone welfare regimes and those of the Scandinavian countries. The difference is that whereas in the Scandinavian countries the labour movement was able to expand the welfare state along decommodifying lines, it was unable to do so in the radical countries. In his comparison of Canadian and US social policies, Myles (1998) offers a solution that retains the liberal label for the Anglo countries but introduces the concept of program design—that is, the models used to finance and distribute benefits—as a way to get at intra-regime variations.

Esping-Andersen's (1990) original snapshot of welfare regimes was taken in the 1980s, a decade marked by the rise of neoliberal discourse in the wake of the oil crises of the 1970s and the advance of 'globalization', which in turn gave rise to a debate on welfare state retrenchment. *Three Worlds* suggests that retrenchment might meet the least resistance in liberal regimes and the most where social democratic logics were well established. Pierson (1996, p. 175) challenged this, arguing that even in liberal regimes, 'maturing social programs produced new organized interests, the consumers and providers of social services, that are usually well-placed to defend the welfare state'. Even though moments of fiscal crisis might open opportunities for reform, such reforms are more likely to be incremental in nature; in other words, they are more likely to follow path-dependent logics. Pierson (1998, p. 554) later went on to argue that while pressures for reform were mounting, they would continue to encounter 'immovable objects' in the form of popular support for social programs, resulting in efforts to restructure and modernize the social contract. As we shall see in Chapter 4, the theme of this sort of 'welfare state recalibration' would come to dominate research as the new millennium dawned (Ferrera and Hemerijck 2003; Palier and Martin 2008; Bonoli and Natali 2012; Morel et al. 2012a).

Gendering welfare regimes

A more fundamental critique of three worlds came from feminist scholars, who argued that his theory emphasized class at the expense of gender.[4] In other words, by focusing on the relationship between (paid) work and welfare, regime theorists underestimated the role played by the family, the gendered nature of the unpaid work performed therein and the consequences for the latter on citizenship. Some feminists sought to construct alternative, gender-based systems for classifying welfare regimes (Lewis 1992; Siaroff 1994; Lewis and Ostner 1995; Sainsbury 1996), while others, notably Orloff (1993a) and O'Connor (1993), engaged with, and sought to gender, three worlds.

Lewis's (1992) original work stressed the centrality of the male breadwinner model to the architecture of all welfare regimes. The work-welfare connection highlights the role of the male breadwinner, typically leaving women to gain what entitlements they could through their dependent status as wives and mothers. Welfare regimes differed, however, in terms of the strength of their focus on the male breadwinner. 'Strong' male breadwinner regimes, like those in Britain and Ireland, institutionalized an inequality between men and women in social security, lacked child care services and rights to maternity or parental leave and thus encouraged, at best, women's part-time participation in paid work. Moderate breadwinner regimes, like that in France, where women's labour force participation had long been higher, recognized women's claims as both wives-mothers and paid workers, but left male authority in the household unchallenged. Unlike both of these regimes, Sweden, with its extensive public child care system, parental leave and individual taxation, was, in the early 1990s, moving towards a dual breadwinner model.

Sainsbury (1996, p. 41) developed an approach for systematically analysing variations in the strength of the male breadwinner model based on 'the type of familial ideology; its influence on social policy in terms of the unit of benefits and contributions and the nature of entitlement; its influence in other policy areas reinforcing the actual division of labor within the family; the boundary between the public and private spheres; and the degree to which women's caring work is paid or unpaid'. For her, there are two ideal types of social policy models—the one centred on the male breadwinner, which was found in both the original liberal and corporatist regimes described above, and that centred on the individual. In the latter, there is no preferred family form but tasks of breadwinning and domestic care are shared in the family. Moreover,

> an essential basis for entitlement is citizenship or residence because it acknowledges that individuals have a variety of useful tasks in life not limited to paid work. It privileges neither earning nor caring and thus accommodates the share tasks of earner and carer ... The boundary between the private and public spheres is fluid. Many reproductive tasks are performed in the public sector. Care, even in the home can be paid work and provide entitlement to social security benefits. (1996, pp. 42–3)

Sainsbury's individual model has much in common with Fraser's (1997) ideal 'dual caregiver model'. For both scholars, it is something to aspire to and exists as a way to critically assess the limitations of all other existing models.

Among feminists who engaged directly with three worlds, Orloff's (1993a) classic essay, 'Gender and the social rights of citizenship: the comparative analysis of gender relations and welfare states', illustrates the benefits of such an encounter. In addition to highlighting the different combinations of state, family and market, Orloff pointed out that stratification also occurs along both gender and class lines. For instance, in liberal regimes, lone mothers frequently constitute the majority of those dependent on means-tested social assistance, while male breadwinners enjoy the higher benefits offered by (corporate or public) social insurance. Esping-Andersen's (1990) emphasis on decommodification poses the most important problem for Orloff and other feminists to the extent that women's primary role remains that of the domestic caregiver. For Orloff (1993a), then, a feminist social democratic regime would (1) ensure women's access to paid work, including the provision of services that enable them to balance work and family life, and (2) support their capacity to form and maintain an autonomous household. O'Connor (1993, p. 511) similarly stresses the need to supplement the concept of decommodification with that of 'personal autonomy or insulation from personal and/or public dependence'. As Lister (1997, p. 173) put it, this involves 'the degree to which individual adults can uphold a socially acceptable standard of living, independent from family relationships, either through paid work or through social security provisions'. Lister (1994), along with McLaughlin and Glendinning (1994), offered a new concept to get at this—defamilialization.

In *Social Foundations of Postindustrial Economies*, Esping-Andersen (1999) responded, proposing the adoption of the concept of 'defamilialization', which is in many respects similar to the feminist version[5] as it focuses on policies that make it possible for individuals to exist 'independently of familial or conjugal reciprocities'. For Esping-Andersen, the Nordic social democratic regime best achieves this since it offers alternative income guarantees to those of the market, unlike liberal regimes that offer meagre, stigmatizing benefits, and provides the services and social insurance (parental leave) that encourage women's full-time, life-long participation in the labour market. He did not, however, broaden his definition of political mobilization to include women's movements, women's units within unions and political parties or women's representation in corporatist bodies, parliament or cabinet.

Feminist scholars have also recognized that there can be important intra-regime differences related to gendered assumptions. O'Connor et al. (1999) thus showed that while the Australian, British, Canadian and US welfare regimes could all be classified as liberal, they exhibited important differences in their gender models. While Australia and Britain are more strongly supportive of the female caregiver, Canada and the Unites States are more open to the adult earner family. Nor were such differences confined to liberal regimes. Bergqvist and her colleagues (1999) thus documented key differences among the Nordic countries, with Norway and Finland more supportive of women as domestic caregivers, while Sweden came closest to supporting the dual breadwinner/dual caregiver model. Yet even the 'familialistic' corporatist regimes exhibited differences, for example, in the public commitment to childcare (Morgan 2006). Recent literature has documented significant movement towards a dual earner model in corporatist regimes long characterized as 'familialistic' (Leitner 2010; Fleckenstein and Lee 2014; Ferragina and Seeleib-Kaiser 2015).

Beyond the Northern core

The majority of comparative work on welfare states (or regimes) focuses on Western Europe, North America and the Antipodes. Thus, the social protection architectures erected in the Soviet bloc were largely ignored, as were the social policy edifices constructed in Latin America, especially in the more developed countries of the region. As a member of the OECD, Japan had received some attention (Goodman and Peng 1996) but Esping-Andersen (1997, p. 188) could dismiss the claim that it constituted a distinct regime, as its 'hybrid' combination of corporatist and liberal features likely reflected its lack of institutional roots. Thus, definition of the Japanese welfare state 'must await the passage of time'.

'Globalization' in all its facets, along with important shifts in the international system—the fall of the Berlin Wall, the rise of the Asian 'tigers' and, more recently, the new weight assumed by the BRICS (that is, the 'emerging' economic powers, Brazil, Russia, India, China and South Africa)—has made it clear that the rest of the world can no longer be ignored. In fact, Hanlon et al. (2013) go so far as to claim that experiments in Brazil, India, China and South Africa are leading the way in the creation of a new social policy paradigm centred on non-contributory cash transfers. For instance, Brazil and Mexico have become known for their social policy innovation of conditional cash transfers (CCTs) for the poor (Fenwick, 2016; Peck and Theodore, 2015). Post-apartheid South Africa has considerably expanded non-contributory social assistance programs such as the Child Support Grant and its non-employment based pension, the Older Person Grant (Clarke 2015, p. 204). China has also expanded health and pension coverage for urban and, more recently, rural citizens (Hong and Kongshøj 2014; Yu 2015). Although inequalities in coverage among different segments of the working population remain a major issue, China has created large social programs, including for those living in rural areas.

India's National Rural Employment Guarantee Scheme similarly aims to improve the conditions of the rural poor. Extension of coverage to those outside the formal sector, especially those living in rural areas, is a critical issue for other lower-income countries, which typically lack adequate social policy coverage for rural populations (Williamson and Béland 2015).

Bringing in these countries and the rest of the world involves more than multiplying the number of welfare regimes. Rather, it raises a number of important questions. First, the triangle of states, markets and families has to be stretched into a diamond, with the fourth point constituted by community/civil society. Second, decommodification poses even more problems for scholars studying regimes outside the Global North than it did for feminists, at least when dealing with countries where many have not been fully incorporated into capitalist relations of production. Third, as in Southern Europe, state and party structures are often conducive to clientelism, whereby social programs are used to buy support for ruling parties. Therefore, de-clientelization might be added to decommodification, stratification and the feminist right to autonomous existence (Wood and Gough 2006). Fourth, incorporating welfare regimes of the South provides an opportunity to revisit the path dependency thesis, especially as many have been subject to deeper and more prolonged crises than those experienced in the North during the 1980s. Finally, it is clearly impossible to treat welfare regimes as if they are solely the product of national forces; the transnational has also to be included. This will be discussed in Chapter 8.

To be sure, others have argued the case for adding a fourth (community/civil society) dimension to the welfare mix (Jenson and Martin 2003). Esping-Andersen (1999, p. 35) himself admitted, albeit in a footnote, that the 'third' sector of voluntary or non-profit provision should be added to the original triad as the latter, 'often run by the Church', plays an important role in countries like Germany and Austria. Wood and Gough (2006), however, argue that inclusion of the community sector is critical to understanding social provision and de facto patterns of rights and obligations in many parts of the South. As they note, community 'represents a wider range of institutional practices between the state and the household involving hierarchy as well as reciprocity, thus inequality and power. It also represents a continuum from immediately local and ascriptive relations . . . to wider, more organized and purposive ones' (Wood and Gough 2006, p. 1702). Moreover, it should not be assumed that the nation state plays a central role in the diamond. While most Northern countries have welfare state regimes, in the South where 'well-functioning labor and financial markets are not pervasive', thus limiting the capacity of the state to compensate for social inequalities, it is preferable to employ the broader concept of welfare regime.

Second, where significant parts of the population have not been directly incorporated into capitalist relations of production, it makes less sense to talk of decommodification. For instance, Filgueira (2005, p. 24) argues that the welfare regimes developed in Brazil and Mexico were 'dualistic' because in parts of both countries, 'there is a virtual exclusionary system with very low incorporation of the vast majority of the population (either through the market or the state)'. In such contexts, the rural peasantry, landless labourers and those making their living in the informal sector have, in a sense, yet to be commodified. Wood and Gough (2006) thus replace Esping-Andersen's decommodification index with the United Nations Development Programme's (UNDP) human development index to develop two new regime types. The first type is informal security regimes, 'institutional arrangements where people rely heavily upon community and family relationships to meet their security needs, to greatly varying degrees'. The second type is insecurity regimes, 'institutional arrangements which generate gross insecurity and block the emergence of stable informal mechanisms to mitigate, let alone rectify, these' (Wood and Gough 2006, p. 1699). The former include parts of Latin America, Southeast and South Asia, and certain countries of sub-Saharan Africa (Wood and Gough 2006, p. 1704), while the majority of the insecurity regimes are found in sub-Saharan Africa, with the exception of South Africa.[6]

Third, as in Southern Europe, in countries lacking an autonomous bureaucracy where elite-dominated parties are predominant, welfare regimes are frequently permeated by clientelism. Filgueira (2005) argues that this was the case in much of Latin America, while Wood and Gough (2006, p. 1699) suggest that such relations are typical of informal security regimes where 'poorer people trade some short-term security in return for longer-term vulnerability and dependence'. The concept de-clientelization should therefore be added to decommodification and stratification. De-clientelization 'refers to the process of de-linking client dependents from their personalized, arbitrary and discretionary entrapment to persons with intimate power over them' and 'to dis-establish clientelist forms of representation and provisioning and establish . . . more formal rights to welfare and security' (Wood and Gough 2006, p. 1708). Thus, one of the claims made by those promoting Mexico's conditional cash transfer program, PROGRESA/ *Oportunidades*, is that it avoided clientelistic political interference that had plagued previous programs such as PRONASOL.[7]

Reflection on welfare regimes outside the old core also suggests the value of revisiting the path dependency thesis. The institutional underpinnings of welfare regimes in Central and Eastern Europe, Latin America and Northeast Asia have been shaken by economic crises and democratization. Historical institutionalism suggests that such events can give rise to critical junctures, opening up the possibility of path-shifting changes. How have these regimes fared?

In Eastern Europe during the communist era, the welfare regimes that were established 'consisted of the provision of highly subsidized prices on food, housing, transport and basic necessities, guaranteed employment, adequate health and education provision and small differentials between the wages of workers, professionals and managers, in return for the political quietude of the population' (Deacon 2000, p. 147). The key access point, however, was through the workplace and, as Deacon (2000, pp. 151–2) notes, these 'could be readily converted into insurance-based, wage-related and differentiated benefit entitlements of the Austro-German, Bismarckian kind'. Writing nearly a decade later, Haggard and Kaufman (2008, p. 341) noted that, on the whole, while there had been some movement in a liberal direction, 'the principles of comprehensive protection that underlay the socialist welfare systems showed surprising resilience in Eastern Europe'. Thus, social insurance covers a relatively broad range of risks and has been supplemented with government financing of uninsured groups, reflecting a continuing commitment to universality (Haggard and Kaufman 2008, p. 341).

There is, however, evidence of some differences in the direction reform takes. Thus, Hacker's (2009) analysis of reforms related to pensions, health care and unemployment led him to suggest that reforms do not always follow a single path. Rather, Central and Eastern European countries are borrowing in various ways from all four worlds, including the Southern European. Their regimes should therefore be classified as hybrid. In terms of defamilialization, former communist regimes fostered women's dual roles as mothers and workers (Pascall and Manning 2000). While Slovenia and Lithuania have continued to support defamilialization, and do so in a manner associated with social democratic regimes, Hungary, the Czech Republic and Estonia have embraced the kind of 'explicit familialism' associated with conservative corporatism, and the withdrawal of support in Poland, Slovakia and Latvia marks a turn towards the 'implicit' familialism associated with liberal approaches (Javornik 2014).

While Esping-Andersen (1997) earlier dismissed the idea of a distinct Asian regime typified by Japan, others have made the case for distinct regimes. Thus, Jones (1993, p. 214) argued for the existence of a distinct 'Confucian' welfare regime characterized by 'conservative corporatism without (Western-style) worker participation; subsidiarity without the church; solidarity without equality; laissez faire without libertarianism . . . "household economies" with states run in a style of a would-be traditional Confucian, extended family'. Holliday (2000) made the case for the existence of a 'productivist' welfare regime in Japan, Hong Kong, Singapore, Korea and Taiwan. Such a regime is characterized by the way that social policy 'is strictly subordinated to the overriding policy objective of economic growth. Everything else flows from this: minimal social rights with extensions linked to productive activities, reinforcement of the position of productive elements in society, and state–market–family relationships directed toward growth' (Holliday 2000, p. 708).

Focusing on Korea and Taiwan, Peng and Wong (2008) suggest, however, that democratization in the 1980s and the Asian financial crisis at the end of the 1990s opened the way to path-shifting reforms. Even while social insurance remained the dominant institutional form, this was expanded in the 1980s to include the self-employed workers in the informal sector and dependents. Also, in the wake of the financial crisis, a new productivist coalition emerged in support not only of skills training and education but also, in response to falling fertility/population ageing, investment in social care and women-friendly workplaces (Peng and Wong 2008, p. 79). In a subsequent article, Peng (2012) argued that Japan was moving in a similar defamilializing direction as Korea. Estévez-Abe and Kim (2014) concur, noting that though both Japan and Korea continue to be marked by familialism, they are in the process of transformation. This is occurring especially rapidly in Korea.

In Latin America, whereas Barrientos (2009) classified pre-crisis regimes in the region as 'conservative-informal', Filgueira (2005) distinguished between the 'stratified universalist' regime (Argentina, Chile, Uruguay and Costa Rica);[8] the dualist regime (Brazil and Mexico); and the exclusionary regime (found in the remaining countries).[9] Clearly, the economic crises, on the one hand, and the political democratization of the 1980s, on the other, had an impact. The emergent regime across the region bore the marks of a 'liberal-informal' regime, 'liberal because of its continued reliance on market provision and hyphenated because of a weakening of the previously strict segmentation in provision' (Barrientos 2009, p. 89). Filgueira (2005, p. 53) was more cautiously optimistic, as the victory of parties of the left/centre left in the early 2000s opened up the possibility of movement towards an embryonic 'basic inclusive universalism'. It would appear that the centre-left governments of Argentina, Brazil, Chile, Costa Rica and Uruguay have indeed been moving in the direction of 'basic universalism' (Huber and Stephens 2012; Pribble 2013).

Not only have (some) Latin American countries responded to the challenges by expanding coverage in key fields, they—or, more specifically, the old 'dualist' regimes of Brazil and Mexico—have also been the site of an important social policy innovation: conditional cash transfers (CCTs). The latter have not only spread across the South (with the help of the World Bank) but also inspired policy changes in the North (Peck and Theodore 2010). Moreover, although Mexico's *Oportunidades* program reinforced rather than undermined familialism (Molyneux 2006), it was designed with the aim of promoting de-clientelization, albeit with somewhat limited success (Luccisano and Macdonald 2012). While Argentina's CCT program remained ensnared in clientelistic politics, Brazil's was more successful since the federal government could get around state governors by enlisting the support of municipalities (Fenwick 2010, 2016).

Conclusion

Considering the above discussion, perhaps Esping-Andersen was right to caution against too firm classifications of the regimes beyond the core. Here we might agree with Powell and Kim's (2014, p. 634) conclusion that 'in contrast to the "frozen landscapes" or "path dependence" of European welfare states, a dynamic perspective suggests that some nations are moving too fast to be captured in regime terms by a static classification'. At the same time, even the 'frozen landscapes' of the Western European corporatist regimes appear to be undergoing significant changes. More broadly, while the concept of welfare regimes may be a useful heuristic device, it is important to remain attentive to the possibility of path-shifting changes.

NOTES

1 For instance, two of the most important social policy journals, *Journal of European Social Policy* (volume 25, number 1) and *Social Policy and Society* (volume 14, number 2), devoted special issues to his contribution.

2 For a more detailed discussion of alternative clusters, see Abrahamson (1999) and Arts and Gelissen (2002).

3 Gal (1996), who makes the case for expanding the membership of the Southern model to include Cyprus, Greece, Israel, Malta and Turkey, places greater emphasis on the presence of a substantial 'shadow' economy that deprives the state of revenues while simultaneously leaving its occupants without official social protection.

4 Many feminists also recognized the intersection of gender with class, race/ethnicity and other aspects of social relations. Of particular importance here was Williams's (1995) groundbreaking work. We shall discuss this aspect in Chapter 7.

5 Albeit with no acknowledgement of its prior use by Lister (1994) or McLaughlin and Glendenning (1994).

6 On the latter, see the special issue of *Social Policy and Administration* (volume 46, number 6) co-edited by Knijn and Patel (2012).

7 While it may have reduced the extent of clientelism, it did not however eliminate it (Luccisano and Macdonald 2012).

8 The latter, however, is described as having developed an 'embryonic social democratic' regime (Filgueira 2005, p. 21). In explaining the forces shaping these regimes, Filgueira highlighted 'the depth and shape of their import substitution industrialisation model, political regimes and actors administering such models and the organization and political character assumed by non-elite sectors' (2005, p. 9).

9 For an additional classification that incorporates the concept of familialism, see Martinez-Franzoni (2008). We shall take up her contribution in Chapter 6.

4 Taking ideas seriously in social policy

The study of the role of ideas is hardly new in social policy research. In the early 1970s, for example, Gaston Rimlinger (1971), a proponent of industrialism, stressed the need for students of welfare state development to pay attention to how ideas can affect key social policy decisions. More than a decade later, John W. Kingdon (1984) explored the role of ideas in US health care policy, while Jane Jenson (1989) wrote about 'societal paradigms' and their influence on pre-World War I French and US labour protection. In addition, as Chapter 2 noted, Daniel Levine (1988) emphasized the impact of cultural ideas and values on welfare state development.

Over the last 15 years, scholarly attention has focused on the potential impact of ideas on welfare state politics, with a particular emphasis on the question of policy change, which has been widely debated in the context of historical institutionalism's traditional emphasis on continuity and path dependence (Chapter 2). In this chapter, we review this literature, with a focus on important ideational concepts such as problem definition, policy paradigms, framing processes, cultural categories, social policy language, the relationship between ideas and institutions and, finally, incremental yet transformative forms of policy change. We show that ideas can play a direct role in social policy change, but their impact is frequently mediated by other factors, especially institutional forces.

Defining ideas

Ideas can be simply defined as the causal and normative beliefs held by social and political actors (Béland and Cox 2011). At the broadest level, ideational processes, which include policy ideas but also cultural beliefs and political ideologies, constitute one of the four main types of explanation in social science and policy research, alongside institutional, structural and psychological explanations (Parsons 2007). Ideas can interact with other factors to produce policy stability or change, but they are not epiphenomena in the sense that they cannot be reduced to other elements; they matter in their own right (Campbell 2004). At the same time, ideas do not simply float in the air. They are typically carried by concrete actors, within and beyond the policy process. As Kingdon (1984) once stated, policy ideas can come from anywhere; sources of new ideas include academics, social movements, think tanks and political parties, among others. Yet the ways in which policy ideas are produced and diffused can vary greatly from one country to the next. For instance, in France, the state is more likely to play a central role in generating policy ideas and expertise, a situation that contrasts with the United States, where private, non-profit think tanks play a much greater role in the policy process (Campbell and Petersen 2011). It is, therefore, only possible to assess the potential impact of ideas on social policy decisions when ideas are understood in their concrete context and in relationship to particular actors and other explanatory factors.

While it is now clear that ideas matter, scholars are currently investigating how they matter within concrete policy processes (Jacobs 2009; Mehta 2011). A first step in doing so involves breaking ideas down into distinct categories, since ideational processes can take many different forms (Béland and Waddan 2015). This is what we do in the next four sections, focusing on problem definitions, policy paradigms, framing processes and cultural categories. These four types of ideational processes do not constitute an exhaustive list of how ideas can matter for social policy stability and change, but the next sections should give the reader a better sense of how ideas take concrete and diverse forms within the social policy process.[1]

Problem definitions

The social construction of policy problems is a key aspect of the policy-making process (Rochefort and Cobb 1994). At the most general level, the analysis of social policy must take into account prevailing beliefs about the perceived problems of the day. Changing definitions of these problems, as well as attempts to push new ones onto the policy agenda, or conversely, to reduce their importance, involve political struggles over the very definition of such problems (Mehta 2011; Stone 1997).

The crystallization of the concept of unemployment in the late nineteenth and early twentieth centuries constitutes one good example of the importance of problem definition. By stressing its involuntary nature, this concept challenged the perception of joblessness as a purely individual and moral issue. Instead, joblessness became a significant collective problem and, as a result, a policy issue worthy of both political attention and state action. Although concrete economic shocks like the Great Depression reinforced the legitimacy of this concept, unemployment is, at least in part, an ideational construction stemming from debates among economists and social reformers (Walters 2000).

Another example of a socially constructed policy problem is the idea of dependency, which has changed meaning several times since the nineteenth century (Fraser and Gordon 1994). In fact, a major contribution of feminist scholars like Fraser and Gordon (1994) has been to draw attention to the close relationship between categorical inequalities and the social construction of policy problems. Thus, their historical analysis of the idea of dependency is closely tied to gendered forms of inequality. Tracing the genealogy of major concepts and perceived problems like unemployment and dependency is thus a major aspect of the growing ideational literature on policy change. Here it is assumed that change is more likely to occur once key actors have identified the problems they seek to address and examined the potential range of solutions.

Policy paradigms

One of the main roles of policy ideas is to reduce policy makers' cognitive uncertainty in times of perceived crisis and, more generally, to provide experts and political actors with reform blueprints grounded in a set of assumptions about how to solve the problems of the day through the use of specific policy instruments (Blyth 2002). Moreover, crises are not understood as mere facts, but also, and more importantly, as social and ideational constructions. For Blyth (2002, p. 10), 'the diagnosis of a situation as a "crisis" by a particular set of ideas is a construction that makes the uncertainty that agents perceive explicable, manageable, and indeed, actionable'. During times of stability, existing institutional settings help actors define their mobilization strategies and their interests (that is, what they see as good for them). In periods of acute uncertainty, however, prevailing institutional frameworks are weakened and political actors frequently turn to new policy ideas to master this uncertainty and redefine their interests and strategies. Once embedded in specific institutional settings, these ideas serve as 'cognitive locks' that are instrumental in reproducing these policy institutions over time. Overall, beyond episodes of crisis, ideational processes help define how actors define their interests in particular institutional and political settings (Jenson 1989; Blyth 2002; Hay 2011).

Policy paradigms play a major role in the design of policy blueprints and the construction of interests. For Peter Hall (1993, p. 279), a policy paradigm is 'a framework of ideas and standards that specifies not only the goals of policy and kind of instruments that can be used to attain them, but also the very nature of the problems they are meant to be addressing'. Paradigms articulate the goals and perceived interests of political actors with the concrete policy instruments meant to address specific problems. In the economic field, Keynesianism and monetarism are good examples of policy paradigms that are relatively coherent sets of assumptions about how to solve the policy problems of the day. Generally, such paradigms are located at the background of major policy debates (Campbell 2004). These economic paradigms have direct implications for social policy. For instance, in the post-World War II era, Keynesianism helped legitimize welfare state expansion in advanced industrial societies. Social policy paradigms centred on concepts such as social inclusion and social investment, to be discussed in Chapter 5, exist alongside, or in opposition to, neoliberal economic paradigms.

Although social policy and economic paradigms have a strong cognitive and technical component, they also order normative goals like competitiveness, equality and social solidarity. In his widely cited article on ideas and policy change, Hall (1993) argues that paradigm shifts only occur when the hierarchy of policy goals held by key policy actors is transformed. Here Hall draws on Thomas Kuhn's (1962) work on scientific paradigms to establish clear distinctions between first and second order change, on the one hand, and third order change, on the other. Thus, for Hall, a paradigm shift or 'third order change' involves a change in the actor's goals that can strongly influence policy development. In contrast, first and second order changes only alter the levels and settings of existing policy instruments and the policy instruments themselves, respectively. For example, in the absence of a major change in social policy goals, an increase in tax rates is a first order change, while the creation of new tax credits is a second order change. First and second order changes can be seen as cases of 'normal policy making', namely, of a process that adjusts policy without challenging the overall terms of a given policy paradigm, much like 'normal science'. In contrast, third order change is likely to reflect a very different process marked by radical changes in the overarching terms of policy discourse associated with a 'paradigm shift'. If first and second order changes preserve existing policy patterns, third order change typically involves a more disjunctive process (Hall 1993, p. 279).

Such a scientific analogy is problematic because the policy-making process is a political rather than purely technocratic affair (Muller 2005). Moreover, beyond its scientific overtones, the concept of paradigm may suggest that the policy ideas experts and political actors hold are coherent philosophical constructions. In this sense, the concept of policy paradigm can be misleading because policy makers generally borrow from different sources to formulate their policy blueprints and address concrete social and economic problems. In the end, the policy assumptions they share do not necessarily take the form of a coherent paradigm (Carstensen 2011; Wincott 2011).

Framing processes

Ideational forces can become political weapons that 'allow agents to challenge existing institutional arrangements and the patterns of distribution that they enshrine' (Blyth 2001, p. 4). Such political and discursive weapons largely correspond to what ideational scholars understand as strategic framing (Béland 2005b; for an alternative perspective, see Schön and Rein 1994 and Somers and Block 2005). Grounded in pre-existing cultural and symbolic repertoires, discursive frames 'appear typically in the public pronouncements of policy makers and their aides, such as sound bites, campaign speeches, press releases, and other very public statements designed to muster public support for policy proposals' (Campbell 1998, p. 394). Yet, as suggested by the social movement literature, career politicians are not the only actors who engage in strategic framing (Benford and Snow 2000). Strategic frames are part of most political battles and the competition between these frames and between the actors using them points to what Tasleem Padamsee (2009) refers to as the 'multiplicity of discourses' present in a society at any given moment.

To illustrate the role of ideological and cultural frames in politics and policy change, one can turn to three of the potential ways they can be mobilized. First, frames can take the form of a public discourse used by specific political actors to convince others that policy change is necessary. This is what political scientist Robert H. Cox calls 'the social construction of the need to reform'.

> In a political environment the advocates of reform need to employ strategies to overcome scepticism and persuade others of the importance of reform. In other words, they must create a frame that changes the collective understanding of the welfare state, because doing so 'shapes the path' necessary to enact reform. (Cox 2001, p. 475)

This means that discursive frames can help convince political actors and the general public that existing policy legacies are flawed and that major reforms should be enacted to solve perceived problems. For example, actors who seek to create new social programs need to convince the public that these programs are legitimate and even necessary.

Second, frames help political actors convince other groups and individuals to join a coalition in support of a concrete proposal or vision for change. As discussed above, ideational processes participate in the construction of interests and the ranking of policy goals. Thus, specific political actors can use strategic frames and political discourse to influence the way other actors see their interests and identify with shared policy goals. From this perspective, policy debates are largely about the construction of interests, policy goals and identities, without which political coalitions can hardly survive. Although concrete quid pro quos between key political actors are a major aspect of coalition building (Bonoli 2000), frames can help sell concrete policy alternatives to the public and build a stronger coalition around them. On the one hand, politicians can 'speak to their base' and argue that the measures they support are consistent with the broad ideological principles that cement their existing coalition. On the other hand, ambiguous policy ideas and proposals can make many different actors believe that they have an interest in supporting a complex measure, which can lead to seemingly paradoxical coalitions (Palier 2005). For instance, when framed by skilful policy entrepreneurs (Kingdon 1984), the concept of solidarity is broad enough to appeal to different constituencies. A classic concept (see Chapter 1), solidarity has a positive valence that, even today, makes it attractive as a 'coalition magnet' (Béland and Cox 2016).

Third, political actors can mobilize framing processes to counter criticism targeting the policy alternatives they support. Discursive blame avoidance strategies (Weaver 1986) can take different forms.

For instance, officials may blame economic cycles for an increase in unemployment to convince the public that their decisions are not at the origin of a negative situation. Policy makers can also frame policy alternatives in a way that diverts attention from their actual divergence from well-accepted political symbols or policy paradigms. For example, since the 1980s, Swedish politicians have referred to social democracy to legitimize forms of social policy change that were closer to neoliberalism than to traditional social democratic ideals (Cox 2004). Blame avoidance frames such as these have a preventive component because political actors use them to shield their proposals from criticism. In the Swedish case, for example, politicians deployed social democratic rhetoric because they knew social democracy was a major source of national pride.

Culture and language

Following the lead of scholars like Levine (1988), discussed in Chapter 2, students of ideational processes and social policy have turned to the analysis of deeply embedded cultural assumptions and categories to explain both political behaviour and policy development (van Oorschot 2007). For example, German sociologist Birgit Pfau-Effinger (2005) argues that cross-national differences in cultural assumptions about the economic, political and social order can explain major social policy variations from one country to another. In her view, cultural values and ideals that are dominant in a particular country 'restrict the spectrum of possible policies of a welfare state' (Pfau-Effinger 2005, p. 4). In his recent work on welfare reform in the United States, Brian Steensland (2008) adopts a similar culturalist perspective to show that the political weight of cultural assumptions prevalent in US society helped prevent the enactment of a potentially transformative social assistance reform in the 1970s.

Profound, historically embedded cultural categories are at the foundation of the very language we use to talk about social policy, which is why turning to the comparative history of social policy concepts and language is so relevant (Béland and Petersen 2014). For instance, it is insightful to explore how terms such as 'welfare' and 'welfare state' have become popular in some countries but contested in others, and how particular concepts used to define social policy problems and programs have different meanings over time. For instance, in the United States, 'welfare' has long been a pejorative term associated with dependency and a host of social problems seemingly created or exacerbated by social assistance (Fraser and Gordon 1994; Steensland 2008).

The dominant understanding of welfare in the United States is related to the history of a particular social program, the Aid to Families with Dependent Children program (AFDC). Over time, this program became a symbol of dependency associated with gendered and racial prejudice. As historian Michal Katz (2008, p. 1) put it, beginning in the 1960s a term that had had a positive meaning in the past became 'a code word for public assistance given mainly to unmarried mothers, mostly young women of color'. In this context, 'welfare' became synonymous with 'dependency', an idea that has long intersected with gendered and racial categories (Fraser and Gordon 1994; Steensland 2008). In 1996, with the explicit aim of fighting 'dependency' towards the state, AFDC was abolished and replaced by a new 'welfare' program that imposes strict time limits on most beneficiaries (Béland and Waddan 2012).

Beyond this example, the discussion of concepts such as social exclusion, new social risks and social investment featured in Chapter 5 further stresses the importance of paying attention to the language we use to talk about social policy problems and solutions. Although the systematic study of social policy language is relatively recent, there is strong evidence that paying close attention to the way we define issues and the terminology we use should become part of mainstream social policy research (Béland and Petersen 2014).

Ideas, institutions and social policy change

Ideas only matter in context, which is why social policy scholars pay close attention to how ideational processes interact with other potential explanatory factors, such as structural forces and institutional logics (Campbell 2004; Parsons 2007). Within the literature on ideas and social policy, for instance, much has been written about the interaction between ideas and institutions in processes of policy change. Particularly well known in this regard is the work of Vivien Schmidt (2002, 2011) on 'discursive institutionalism', which focuses on how different types of reform discourse are related to specific political institutions. On the one hand, single-actor systems such as the United Kingdom, where elected officials are the primary source of policy decisions, feature the domination of 'communicative discourse' aimed at convincing the public to support the government in power. On the other hand, multi-actor institutional systems such as Germany, where elected officials must seek agreements with business and labour actors in order to reform social programs, feature the domination of 'coordinative discourse' aimed at forging alliances among these players so that they can coordinate their actions to being about meaningful policy change (Schmidt 2002).

This approach to political discourse is quite different from that of Michael Foucault (1980) and those who employ his governmentality approach, which focuses on the disciplinary power of discourse that, together with techniques of surveillance that form part of the contemporary welfare state, govern not only the poor but also the entire population. Thus, from their perspective, the development of the welfare state is associated not with progress but with increasingly sophisticated forms of social control (Dean 1996, p. 79; for a good overview, see Lister 2010, Chapter 4).

Another way institutions can interact with ideas is when existing policy legacies feature enduring cultural and ideological categories that make change more difficult to achieve. This is because policy makers frame new policy proposals using categories and languages associated with unpopular policies of the past (Steensland 2008). Ideas of the past are embedded in institutions, which tend to promote stability over time (Béland and Cox 2011). Yet in a context of changing demographic and economic circumstances, negative feedback effects from existing policies may weaken these policies over time. This is the case when pension programs created in favourable demographic conditions face major internal challenges as these conditions deteriorate, generating pressures for policy change (Weaver 2010).

Although social policy ideas can promote stability, most of the welfare state literature emphasizing how ideas matter stresses their potential role in bringing about policy change. Such changes can take the form of sudden paradigm shifts (Hall 1993), or incremental, yet transformative patterns such as layering (when new policies are introduced alongside old ones), conversion (when old policies are reframed to take a new meaning) and policy drift (when new socio-economic trends alter the impact and meaning of existing policies). Those who have developed concepts like conversion, layering, and policy drift, such as Jacob Hacker (2004) and Kathleen Thelen (2004; see also Streeck and Thelen 2005a and Mahoney and Thelen 2009) do not see these as strongly related to ideational processes. Yet there is strong evidence that layering is about the implementation of new policy ideas that challenge existing policy institutions, conversion is largely about framing processes, and policy drift is related to changing economic assumptions. The latter may drive the behaviour of employers in a new direction that clashes with existing public social programs. This is why it is clear that to grasp these forms of incremental yet transformative social policy change, it is necessary to pay close attention to policy ideas and the actors formulating and carrying them (Béland and Waddan 2012).

Conclusion

Ideas are only part of the puzzle of social policy change, and ideational processes frequently interact with factors such as economic change, political institutions and business or labour power to shape policy paths and bring about welfare state stability or change. From this perspective, studying the role of ideas is not about focusing only on ideas. Yet it is legitimate to bring these factors to the centre of the ongoing debate about social policy change, which seeks to account for the varying impact of multiple factors over time. Ideas are only one of these factors but we should pay attention to them since they can be significant in different ways, some of which are outlined above.

NOTE

1 The following sections are largely adapted from Béland (2009).

5 Social exclusion, new social risks and social investment

In Chapter 4, we emphasized the need for scholars to properly define and trace the development of key concepts at the core of our ever-changing social policy language. In this chapter, we focus on three concepts that are central to contemporary social policy debates: social exclusion, new social risks, and social investment. While the first two concepts aim to define emerging challenges to which the welfare state should adapt, social investment attempts to reframe the relationship between social and economic policy in response to the challenges posed by neoliberalism—a set of ideas that has celebrated laissez-faire, pro-market policies since the late 1970s and early 1980s. The main objective of this chapter is to trace the development of these three concepts and critically examine their place in contemporary social policy discourse and scholarship. The first section deals with social exclusion, the second with new social risk and the third with social investment, which has emerged as one of the most influential concepts in current international debates about the future of social programming around the world.

Social exclusion

The concept of social exclusion is not a purely academic construction as it has been used widely in policy discourse for over two decades. During this time it has taken on many different meanings (Silver 1994, 2015; Hills et al. 2002; Gallie et al. 2003; Silver and Miller 2003; Béland 2007). Such ambiguous concepts are especially prone to coalition-building efforts on the part of policy entrepreneurs who seek to gather support for their policy solutions (Palier 2005). To understand the meaning of the concept of social exclusion, it is helpful to begin with its historical development, before examining its transnational diffusion, which is a key issue when dealing with most social policy concepts (Béland and Petersen 2014).

The concept of social exclusion first emerged in France, a country where the expansion of the post-war welfare state, which had coincided with almost three decades of economic prosperity, ended with the 1973 oil crisis and stagflation that followed in its wake.[1] The concept emerged first in academic discourse during the last of these three decades of prosperity.[2] Although the terms appeared as early as in 1965 (Klanfer 1965), its origins are usually traced to a 1974 book by René Lenoir (Frétigné 1999).

First in France and later beyond its borders, social exclusion is associated with lack of social integration and limited access to the labour market in a context marked by the spread of long-term unemployment and growing concerns about racism and discrimination. Although evidence suggests that there is no strong relationship between unemployment and social isolation (Gallie et al. 2003), in France, the belief that long-term unemployment and the resulting social exclusion represent a major threat to social order features prominently in the discourse about the deprived suburbs. To a certain extent, the suburbs' geographical isolation reinforced the idea that France was experiencing the emergence of a divided society, an idea that was at odds with the universalistic model of solidarity and social integration that constituted the core of France's republican political tradition (Silver 1994; Béland and Hansen 2000). Economic and urban problems bred ethnic tensions as the portion of the population of African descent felt increasingly left behind. At the same time, fuelled by the emergence of the far-right Front National party,[3] negative stereotypes found fertile ground in the wider populace (Schain 2008, p. 75).

Beginning in the mid to late 1980s, the concept of social exclusion spread beyond France to the rest of Europe. At that time, Jacques Delors, then president of the European Commission, advocated for a stronger 'social dimension' to European integration. Clearly, as a French economist and politician, Delors had been exposed to the concept of social exclusion and, as a policy entrepreneur, he used his position as president of the European Commission to promote the concept in a quest for something that became known as Social Europe (Mahon 2002, p. 362). In 1990 these efforts bore fruit with the creation of the European Observatory on Policies to Combat Social Exclusion (Leney 1999, p. 38). The fight against social exclusion thus gradually became a European policy concept transcending purely academic discourse, just as it had in France (Béland 2007). The 2000 Lisbon and Nice European Councils reinforced this commitment, making it a major feature of the European social welfare agenda, especially with regard to employ-ment policy (Begg and Berghman 2002; van Berkel and Hornemann Møller 2002). The 'fight against exclusion' was thus incorporated into the European Union's use of the 'open method of coordination',[4] and numerous reports on the topic have been produced by the European Union and other European organizations (Fernández de la Hoz 2001; ECORYS 2011).

Social exclusion also rapidly became a central policy concept in a number of European countries. In Britain, for example, the advent of the Third Way and, more specifically, the 1997 electoral victory of New Labour, pushed the issue of social exclusion to the centre of the policy agenda (Levitas 1999 [2005]). The concept of social exclusion has sub-sequently made its way around the world aided in no small part by its adoption by organizations like the World Bank (2013).

Despite the many shades of meaning it has acquired as it travels across the globe, there are at least two things that distinguish the concept of social exclusion from other concepts, such as poverty (Béland 2007). First, social exclusion emphasizes the multifaceted nature of social disadvantage embedded in the individual stories of people who cope with issues including discrimination, lack of opportunities and long-term unemployment (Goguel d'Allondans 2003, p. 43). Second, social exclusion is generally grounded in a horizontal and spatial model rather than the vertical approach associated with income inequality and social stratification. From this angle, people are 'in' or 'out' of the mainstream economy and society as much as they are 'up' or 'down' on the income distribution scale. As a result, income inequality can slip to the margins of the policy agenda (Béland, 2007), at least when social exclusion becomes part of a Third Way approach as it did during the Blair years in the United Kingdom, where the quest for social inclusion favoured a push for regressive forms of activation that ended genuine forms of social entitlement (Dwyer 2004).[5] This understanding of social exclusion is compatible with moderate interpretations of neoliberalism that are grounded in the assumption that the state should fight depri-vation but not income inequality, because the latter is understood as a precondition for economic prosperity (Béland 2007).

Yet, when used more rigorously in conjunction with concepts such as poverty and income inequality, social exclusion can be a sociologi-cally insightful concept for social policy scholars. As the literature on social policy language teaches us, however, social policy concepts can have different meanings that are typically contested within the political arena (Béland and Petersen 2014). Thus, social exclusion can be used as a progressive concept justifying innovative forms of social protection or a conservative concept that legitimizes moralizing forms of activation (Levitas 1999 [2005]). Scholars using social policy concepts like social exclusion that are central to mainstream political discourse have to be particularly careful to rigorously define what they mean by them (Béland 2007).

New social risks

The concept of new social risks are of more recent vintage than social exclusion (Esping-Andersen et al. 2002; Taylor-Gooby 2004; Bonoli 2005; Armingeon and Bonoli 2006; Hacker 2006). For instance, while a search for 'social exclusion' finds more than 285,000 hits on Google Scholar, a similar search for 'new social risks' yields barely 3200 hits.[6] New social risks is also more of a purely academic concept than social exclusion and is more popular with scholars and policy researchers than with politicians and policy makers. Its meaning is also broader than social exclusion as it refers to a wider array of trends and processes.

The concept of new social risks is thus an umbrella concept that subsumes a variety of ongoing social and economic trends that are likely to shape social policy change in the years to come (Bonoli 2005). In a seminal volume, Peter Taylor-Gooby (2004, pp. 2–3) defined new social risks as 'the risks that people now face in the course of their lives as a result of the economic and social changes associated with the transition to a post-industrial society'. For Taylor-Gooby (2004, pp. 3–4), these new social risks arise as the result of four major developments: (1) the movement of women into paid work in ever larger numbers, making it harder for them to balance work and family life, especially those with lower skills; (2) 'the increase in the absolute and relative numbers of elderly people', which contributes to rising demand for health and long-term care; (3) labour market changes that tighten 'the link between education and employment', exacerbating 'the risk of social exclusion among those with poor education'; and (4) the ongoing privatization of social services, which 'can generate new risks when citizen-consumers commit themselves to unsatisfactory choices, and when regulation of standards in private provision is ineffective'. The extent and nature of these new social risks varies greatly from country to country. For instance, social democratic welfare regimes are in a better position to reduce risks associated with work and family balance issues than Mediterranean countries, where affordable public child care remains in short supply (Taylor-Gooby 2004).

For Giuliano Bonoli (2005), new social risks exert pressures on welfare states to create new social programs in response to these very risks. Yet, as Bonoli (2005) suggests, there is no automatic translation of new social risks into innovative policies aimed at tackling these risks. Such policies may not appeal to the industrial, working class constituencies who were the primary beneficiaries of programs developed in the post-war decades, while those that stand to benefit from the new policies constitute a diverse group—youth, low-skilled workers and women. Bonoli (2005) argues that when the interests of these groups, which typically have limited power resources on their own, converge with those of employers, they have a much better chance of seeing governments enacting policies to protect workers against the new social risks outlined above.

The key message of the new social risks literature is thus that welfare states are adapting to changing economic, social and demographic circumstances. Even though some of these risks are not really 'new', this literature does identify certain important trends that both scholars and policy makers need to pay direct attention to in a rapidly changing world. At the same time, old social risks, such as unemployment and poverty in old age, remain a major source of concern (Jenson 2004). In other words, contemporary welfare states need to simultaneously address both older and newer challenges (Béland 2010a). In the absence of such efforts, policy drift can give rise to very negative consequences for citizens, workers and families (Hacker 2006).

Social investment

Widely debated inside and outside academia, social investment is a social policy concept that can be seen as a way to find a new economic legitimacy to social programs (Esping-Andersen 2002; Jenson 2009, 2010; Morel et al. 2012b; Mahon 2013). From the 1930s to the 1970s, the Keynesian policy paradigm provided a strong economic justification for social programs because they were understood to be playing a positive role in economic regulation, especially during downturns when social benefits helped to maintain consumption. This view of social programs began to change in the wake of the 1973 oil crisis and the rise of neoliberalism, spearheaded by the electoral victories of Margaret Thatcher in the United Kingdom and Ronald Reagan in the United States. In new economic and political contexts, as President Regan famously said, government becomes the problem and social spending comes to be seen as an economic burden and an obstacle to prosperity and balanced budgets. Although neoliberalism did not, in fact, lead to the dismantling of the welfare state (Pierson 1994), it did erode support for it among economists and the politicians they advise (Blyth 2002).

Social investment, a social policy concept that began to emerge on the global policy stage in the mid 1990s, seeks to offer an alternative perspective on the relationship between economic prosperity and social programs (Jenson 2009). Rather than depicting social programs as a pure cost for the economy, as traditional neoliberal thinkers do, social investment suggests that in a so-called knowledge society, investment in human capital (training and education) and social programs like universal access to child care and early childhood education are good for the economy. For instance, while access to free or affordable child care promotes social goals such as gender equality, it also has the advantage of increasing women's labour force participation in an era when accelerated demographic ageing is giving rise to labour shortages (Esping-Andersen et al. 2002). At the broadest level, for proponents of social investment, it is possible to have the social cake and eat it too given that early-childhood education and social programs that foster activation and raise skill levels are good for society and for the economy. As Morel et al. (2012b) argue, social investment attempts to fight neoliberalism through a discourse that establishes a positive sum game between economic growth and social well-being. Others, however, see social investment as an extension of, rather than an alternative to, neoliberalism (Craig and Porter 2004; on this debate, see Mahon 2013). Clearly, like social exclusion, social investment is an ideologically ambiguous concept that means different things to different people (on ambiguity see Palier 2005).

As Jenson (2009, p. 448) notes, 'One of the innovations of the social investment perspective is that ideas about gender differences and circumstances as well as the unequal gendering effects of employment and family life are front and center in this policy discourse'. Because social investment challenges traditional gender roles, promotes greater labour market participation among women and justifies greater public investment in child care, feminist scholars such as Jenson (2009) have played a major role in highlighting the concept of social investment, both within and outside academia. Nevertheless, one of the best-known proponents of the social investment perspective, Gøsta Esping-Andersen (2002, 2009), pays scant attention to feminist scholarship on social policy. This is not a unique situation, especially as child-centric approaches to social investment tend to sideline the issue of gender equality (Jenson 2009).

Although the concept of social investment is new, it arguably finds a forerunner in Sweden's post-war economic and social policy model. In fact, Morel and her colleagues (2012b, p. 3) trace it back to the ideas of Alva and Gunnar Myrdal who, in the 1930s, developed 'a new conception of social policy oriented towards the efficient organisation of production and reproduction ... which viewed social policy as an investment rather than a cost'. Such an investment would take the form of public expenditure to ensure an adequate supply of child care, education and health care, thus raising the quality of life for the whole population. The addition of the Rehn-Meidner economic policy model, which combined active labour market policy and solidaristic wage bargaining, added to this by helping to renew the economic structure while enabling displaced workers to qualify for new jobs (Martin 1979; Bonoli 2012, pp. 189–90). In this model, however, there was also support for maintaining investment in human capital not only through active labour market policies but also through social programs such as unemployment insurance (Morel et al. 2012b, p. 4).

Moving beyond its Scandinavian origins, it is important to keep in mind that, like social exclusion, social investment has become a global policy concept; elements of the social investment perspective have been adopted in such diverse regions as the European Union and Latin America (Jenson 2010). International organizations such as the Organisation for Economic Co-operation and Development (OECD) have played an important part in the global diffusion of social investment as a policy idea, a point that will be picked up in Chapter 8. A strong proponent of social investment, the OECD's social policy division began to explore the idea in the wake of the 1970s oil crisis and has acted as a major proponent of the concept since the late 1990s (Mahon 2014). As Mahon (2013) suggests, there are two broader, competing interpretations of the OECD's social investment discourse: one version that is compatible with neoliberal economic policies and one that follows a social democratic approach that is more ambitious and universalistic in nature.

This example shows that the concept of social investment, just like that of social exclusion, can take on different meanings for, and can appeal to, different constituencies. In other words, the multiple or 'polysemic' meanings of such concepts allow them to become appealing coalition-building tools (Palier 2005; Jenson 2010; Béland and Cox 2016). Although such ambiguity can be politically advantageous, it is again rather problematic from both a policy and a scholarly perspective. At the policy level, ambiguous objectives rarely make effective policies. More importantly, lack of clear objectives further complicates policy evaluation, which is typically about assessing whether existing programs have achieved their goals (Mossberger and Wolman 2003, p. 433). Thus, when dealing with social investment and the other concepts discussed in this chapter, social policy scholars need to make sure the concepts they use are clear, empirically grounded, and not easily subject to political and ideological manipulation (Béland and Petersen 2014).

Conclusion

Paying close attention to major social policy concepts and their changing political interpretations, as well as following their international diffusion, is a crucial component of social policy research (Béland and Petersen 2014). In this chapter, we discussed the development of three relatively recent social policy concepts. Social exclusion and social investment are clearly global concepts that have been used widely both within and outside academia. New social risks is a concept more often used in academic circles to encourage social policy scholars to think about how changing demographic, economic and social conditions affect welfare state change. In this sense, the new social risks approach is similar to the industrialism thesis discussed in Chapter 2. As Bonoli (2005) suggests, however, we cannot take politics out of new social risks, at least when we explore the way in which they contribute to social policy change, since such change comes about through collective action, coalition building and, ultimately, power struggles over the changing role of the state. For social exclusion and social investment, politics is more at the fore given that governments and international organizations such as the European Union, the OECD and the World Bank have used these two concepts as rallying cries to bring about policy change in a host of countries, both in the developed and the developing world (Béland 2007; Jenson 2010; Mahon 2013).

As political constructions, social policy concepts are not only about framing reality and scholarly research but also about shaping agenda-setting processes that are integral to the process of welfare state change. This takes place through what Cox (2001) calls 'the social construction of the need to reform'. Over the years and perhaps for decades to come, it is likely that concepts such as social exclusion and social investment will continue to play a direct role in major policy debates about 'who gets what, when and how' (Lasswell 1936).

NOTES

1 This section draws on Béland (2009).

2 On the history of the idea of exclusion in France, see Goguel d'Allondans (2003) and Silver (1994).

3 On the Front National, see Goodliffe (2012).

4 The open method of coordination 'is a method of soft governance which aims to spread best practice and achieve convergence towards EU goals in those policy areas which fall under the partial or full competence of Member States' (European Parliament 2014, p. 1).

5 On the idea that the discourse on social exclusion is related to a decline of concerns about income inequality at large, especially the one between middle and upper class, see Hills (2004).

6 Social investment, the last of these three concepts, is much more widely used in academic discourse than new social risks, but is used much less than the older concept of social exclusion, with about 41,000 hits on Google Scholar. These online searches were conducted in February 2015 using the Google Scholar online portal: http://scholar.google.com.

6 Changing gender norms, welfare regime forms

As the last century drew to a close, the male breadwinner–female caregiver norm that underpinned post-war welfare state regimes came under increasing pressure. The shift from industrial goods production to service-centred economies increased opportunities for women's employment just as the move to deregulate labour markets was making it more difficult for men to earn enough to play the role of breadwinner. Demographic developments (that is, falling fertility rates and population ageing) in turn lent credence to new social policy ideas like those discussed in Chapter 5. Just as importantly, second wave feminism advanced the case for women's 'equal economic opportunity' while the United Nations Decade for Women helped to make gender equality a global norm. Together, these developments prompted a series of 'farewells to maternalism' (Orloff 2006) and the ushering in of the adult worker family norm. How have welfare states responded to the challenges this has posed and what factors have shaped states' responses? How best can we assess policy responses in terms of their contribution not only to gender but also to racial/ethnic and class equality?

We begin this chapter with a critical reflection on the concept of 'defamilialization' coined by feminists like Lister (1994) and popularized by Esping-Andersen (1999) to capture a (potential) direction policy change could take. Is this concept the best way to grasp the complexity of these changes, including their implications for gender equality? The next section asks to what extent responses to the challenge of changing family forms are determined by the structure of existing welfare regimes. That is, how important is path dependency? Scandinavian social democracies are considered 'pioneers' in regard to defamilialization and gender equality, while countries with corporatist welfare regimes have been described as inhibited from responding to such a challenge by their familialistic underpinnings. Are they indeed 'frozen'? If not, what are the driving forces behind path-altering changes? The final section takes us to one of the major areas of new research in this field—the emergence of transnational 'care chains' involving the movement of care workers from poorer areas in the South (or East) to look after young children, the invalid and the frail elderly in the homes of families and in care institutions in wealthier countries.

Defamilialization?

One way welfare state theorists attempt to capture the nature and extent of changes in gender norms is through the concept of 'defamilialization', popularized by Esping-Andersen (1999). For Esping-Andersen (1999, p. 45), defamilialization was designed to identify social policies 'that lessen individuals' reliance on the family; that maximize individuals' command of economic resources independently of familial or conjugal reciprocities'. This definition, as Orloff noted (2009, p. 320, footnote 6), lacked the critical edge given by the feminist scholars who had originally coined the term. For feminists, defamilialization sought to capture the extent to which policies contribute to altering the balance of power between men and women and 'hence the *terms and conditions under which people engage in familial or caring arrangements*' (Lister 1994, p. 29, emphasis added). In addition to focusing on power relations, the second definition highlights the important work of care, who provides it and under what conditions. In fact, for feminists like Jenson (1997) and Daly and Lewis (2000), 'care' ought to be at the centre of our attempts to theorize the direction of welfare state redesign.

More broadly, and central to defamilialization as Esping-Andersen defined it, is a process of 'individualization' fostered by policies that encourage and support the employment of both parents, thereby creating the adult earner family, through changes to taxation and social security programs that make the individual, not the family, the operative unit. Interpreted this way, defamilialization can be seen as central to the commodification of women (that is, women as labour market participants) and to the commodification, or at least monetization, of their former domestic caring duties. To be sure, feminists like O'Connor (1993) and Orloff (1993a) had been critical of Esping-Andersen for overlooking the way that women's participation in paid work could lessen their dependence on, and hence subordination to, men within the family. Yet for Esping-Andersen's intellectual mentor, Polanyi, family constituted part of that network of reciprocal relationships that served to 'embed' labour. In the absence of such networks of support, labour is simply a commodity. Similarly, defamilialization can strip women of former protections through the reduction or elimination of lone mothers' claims to benefits, while 'familializing' programs such as pension credits for periods spent caring decommodify care work (Daly 2011, p. 9). In other words, it is important to explore more carefully what is involved in the process of defamilialization.

Of course, the state (or the voluntary sector or the market) can take over some of the functions previously supplied by women's (unpaid) labour, providing services that substitute for it, but only partially. As Saraceno and Keck (2010, p. 677) argue, defamilialization can never be total nor does it 'stand in contrast to family and intergenerational feelings of responsibility and solidarity'. In other words, the idea of the family/household involves something more than a set of functional arrangements. As Daly and Lewis (2000, p. 290) note,

> In social Catholicism . . . a philosophy that underpins to varying degrees all the continental southern European welfare states, the giving and receiving of care is part of the normal reciprocity between individuals who are defined by the nature of their embeddedness in a range of social relations . . . Family solidarity was understood as a readiness to care (as well as to provide cash) for one another.

While this particular family norm indeed presumed the subordination of women within a patriarchal household, at the same time, this quotation highlights the important normative framework that surrounds the provision and receipt of care. Or, as theorists of the ethic of care would argue, caring labour entails a large 'non-commodified human element' (Radin 1996, p. 105) made all the more complex by the human relationships involved.

What feminists were arguing for, therefore, was 'relational autonomy' between the caregiver and the recipient of care. On the one hand, this entails respect for the rights of the recipient. On the other, as Lewis (2008, p. 276) put it,

> if care is a universal human need . . . it has to be possible for anyone to choose to do it, as a matter of both principle and pragmatic policy making. For, given that informal care usually involves emotion and love as well as labour and passive 'watching over' . . . policy must make it possible to exercise what Sen . . . terms 'real agency freedom'—a genuine choice to do care work.

Such a possibility involves support for one's decision to provide care, such as (income-related) leaves for child or elder care, as well as the possibility of at least partially opting out (for example, through access to publicly provided and/or subsidized child and elder care services).[1]

This more nuanced position is reflected in the models developed by Leitner (2003) and Saraceno and Keck (2010). The former's typology includes 'optional familialism', where 'services as well as supportive care policies are provided. Thus, the caring family is strengthened but is also given the option to be (partly) unburdened from caring responsibilities' (Leitner 2003, p. 359). Saraceno and Keck (2010, p. 676) identify three broad strategies: familialism by default, 'when there are neither publicly provided alternatives to, nor financial support for, family care'; supported familialism, 'when policies, usually through financial transfers—including taxation and paid leaves—support (specific) family members in keeping up their financial and care responsibilities'; and defamilialization, 'when individualization of social rights (for example, with regard to minimum income provision, or entitlement to higher education or to receiving care) reduces family responsibilities and dependencies'. For Saraceno and Keck (2010), a combination of the latter two can offer the best set of arrangements supporting an earner–carer norm, but only if there are sufficient incentives for parents to share familial care.

The literature on the emerging adult earner family recognizes one important set of changes in the nature of families, while feminists underline the importance not only of equality between men and women in the world of paid work but also in the division of unpaid familial labour. This work needs to go further, however, to grapple with important differences between caring for young children, persons with disabilities and the elderly. As Saraceno and Keck (2010, p. 691) point out, 'children and the elderly have a different legal and social status. Individualization of entitlement is greater for the latter than the former. Furthermore, young children may not be totally and not even largely defamilialized without depriving them of the possibility to develop meaningful and loving relationships'. Much of the literature on defamilialization and care focuses on care arrangements for young children. In scholarship and in practice, the care needs of the elderly and dependent adults in general have been less well addressed.[2] It is as if their very individualization has resulted in the failure to acknowledge their care needs (Saraceno and Keck 2010, p. 693).

The literature also needs to recognize the diversity of family forms. Thus, gay and lesbian couples have fought for recognition of equal rights to those accorded heterosexual families. The increase in single-person households, often embedded in a network of friends, also suggests that such non-familial ties also need recognition. Leitner's (2003, p. 368) distinction between gendered and de-gendered familialism aptly captures these dimensions. The first involve

> family policies that assign family care to women (or men) only, devalue family care in relation to employment, do not provide choices to (re-)move from family care to employment, and focus on the (married) heterosexual couple family. Contrarily, de-gendered familialism shows familialistic family policies that do not refer to biological sex differences, validate family care, enable the financial independence of the carer, provide choices to move between family care and employment, and provide comparable benefits for different family arrangements.

This vision of the earner–carer family has much in common with Nancy Fraser's (1997, pp. 59–62) 'universal caregiver' paradigm, a gender equal ideal in which unpaid care work, as well as involvement in the associational life of civil society, is treated on par with the world of paid work.

Towards an adult earner family norm?

Theorists of the new social risks discussed in Chapter 5, such as Esping-Andersen (1999) and Bonoli (2006), initially predicted that social democratic and liberal regimes would facilitate the emergence of the adult earner family, albeit via different routes. While the first would offer publicly financed care services, the second would encourage the formation of (often low wage) markets for care. Thus, countries with social democratic regimes like Sweden have pioneered provision of universal child and elder care services and parental leave while those with liberal regimes like Canada and the US have largely relied on markets. There are, however, significant differences among countries with the same kind of regime. Among the Nordic countries, Finland and to a lesser extent Norway support longer child care leaves and, while all Nordic countries offer paid parental leave, they differ in length and generosity of compensation. Moreover, only Norway, Sweden and Iceland reserve a portion of paternal leave for the father, the so-called 'daddy quotas' (Ellingsaeter 2014). Among the Anglo-American countries, while the

US has no paid maternal or parental leave program, Canada offers paid parental leave, and its francophone province of Quebec includes a daddy quota. In addition, as O'Connor and her colleagues (1999) argue, although both Australia and Britain have liberal welfare regimes, both continue to support the female caregiver.

New social risks theorists predicted that conservative regimes would shore up the male breadwinner-female caregiver family form. Yet, since the dawn of the twenty-first century, there has been significant movement away from the traditional breadwinner family norm, even in countries where this remained dominant right to the end of the twentieth century. To what extent have policies such as parental leave, daddy quotas and child care supported a movement towards the earner–carer family form? How can we account for processes of change (and continuity)?

In the field of child care,[3] Morgan (2009, p. 42) notes that 'More generally, states seem to be moving toward a model of extensive leave time, coupled with publicly subsidized child care that is available after the long leave, followed by reduced work hours'. This is also the case in countries that had previously based their social policies on the male breadwinner, including liberal ones like the UK (Fleckenstein and Seeleib-Kaiser 2011), those with conservative regimes like Germany and Austria (Fleckenstein and Seeleib-Kaiser 2011; Fleckenstein and Lee 2014), Asian countries like Japan and Korea (Peng 2011) and the wealthier countries of Latin America (Staab and Gerhard 2010; Faur 2011). That said, progress remains uneven (Leitner 2010; Estévez-Abe and Kim 2014; Lopreite and Macdonald 2014; Oliver and Mätzke 2014).

Clearly, child and elder care services can support the adult earner family, though it is also important to consider whether such support targets low-income families (as it does in the UK, for instance) and whether public subsidies focus on the supply (Nordic) or demand (UK, Canada and Australia) side (Mahon et al. 2016). The adoption of paid parental leave can also support the adult earner family but it is policies designed to get fathers to share domestic care responsibilities, such as a daddy quota, that constitute a key indicator of a commitment to an earner–carer model. Ray and her colleagues (2010) built this proviso into their 'gender equality index' for assessing the implications of leave programs. Despite their importance for gender equality, however, daddy quotas remain a contested issue even within the

Nordic countries (Ellingsaeter 2014; Bergqvist et al. 2015). Nor have neo-maternalist solutions such as long child care leaves been limited to the corporatist countries. Child care allowances for extended periods following parental leave have been adopted in Finland, Norway and Sweden (Eydal and Rostgaard 2011).

Thus, it is primarily women who take the leave and women who work part time because domestic care largely continues primarily to be women's responsibility. This, in turn, works against equality in the labour market as it leads to deepening occupational segregation and the hardening of the 'glass ceiling', both of which are very visible in Sweden, one of the countries where social policies have in many ways gone the furthest towards supporting an earner–carer model (Orloff 2006; Lister 2009; Morgan 2009). In other words, rather than supporting an earner–carer family, for the most part, these policies support the emergence of the 'one and a half earner family' (Mahon 2002; Daly 2011).

How have various authors attempted to explain these patterns of continuity and change? Esping-Andersen (1999) and Korpi (2000) argue that power resource theory, with its emphasis on parties of the left and unions, accounts for how and why the Nordic 'social democratic' countries pioneered this course, while Mahon (1997), Bergvqvist and her colleagues (1999) and Huber and Stephens (2006) would add the role played by feminists. However, in her account of failures to fully institutionalize the earner–carer norm, even in the Nordic countries, Morgan (2009, p. 46) suggests that while feminists have helped to create political pressures for reform, they have nowhere been in a position to determine the precise features of the new policies.

Fleckenstein and Seeleib-Kaiser (2011) agree that power resource theory can account for the pioneers, but argue that it is less helpful in accounting for important changes—and differences between them—in Germany and Britain since 2000. Instead they build on the Varieties of Capitalism approach, arguing that the types of policies adopted reflect the distinctive character of the post-industrial skill profiles of the two countries, which in turn shape the attitude of business towards child care and leave programs. In developing their argument, they also draw on Korpi's (2006) distinction between protagonists, consenters and antagonists, adding a fourth category of actor, 'promotors', who rank a policy among their first order preferences 'but are not involved in the initial agenda setting' (Fleckenstein and Seeleib-Kaiser 2011,

p. 141). Thus, business may not have been the protagonist in Britain or in Germany, but it played a key promoter role in both countries.

In accounting for the embrace of policies to reconcile work and family life by centre-right parties, Leitner (2010) and Fleckenstein and Lee (2014) focus on the impact of party competition in the context of the electorate's changing (post-industrial) preferences, while Da Roit and Sabatelli (2013) explain the mismatch between growing needs and Italian child care policies in part by the lack of party competition. In addition, harking back to Ferrera's (1996) analysis of the South European model discussed in Chapter 3, Da Roit and Sabatelli (2013, p. 444) highlight the weakness of the Italian state and the clientelism that permeates its bureaucracy. State structures and policy legacies also feature in Wincott's (2006) account of patterns of provision in the United Kingdom post-devolution, Oliver and Mätzke's (2014) comparison of Germany and Italy, and Mahon and Brennan's (2013) comparison of child care and parental leave policies in Australia and Canada.

All of the above accounts draw on historical institutionalism. Estévez-Abe and Kim (2014, pp. 669–70), however, develop an approach based on rational choice institutionalism to explain why Korea has been able to implement child and elder care reforms more rapidly than Japan. They argue that reforms are likely to proceed more rapidly where there are 'open political opportunity structures':[4]

> [A] political system capable of addressing new issues or responding to needs of groups not previously part of the policy circle. Such structures emerge when there are institutions that: 1) make political leaders sensitive to new social needs; and 2) enable them to set the new policy agenda and control the legislative processes. (p. 669)

In contrast, closed political opportunity structures are those 'where political leaders are not sensitive to new social needs, or cannot set the agenda even if they are'. While the authors apply these concepts to Japan and Korea, they could also be useful in contexts such as that described by Da Roit and Sabatelli (2013) above, where there is growing evidence of a gap between the need for care services and the state's response.

Policy ideas of the sort discussed in Chapter 5 also figure in these accounts. The current interest in social investment helps to account for convergence tendencies in the field of child care policy. Thus, Peng (2011) considers the impact of social investment ideas on Korean policy makers while Mahon and her colleagues (2012) consider the diverse ways in which national actors have drawn on social investment and neoliberal ideas to guide their reforms. Such ideas may and do travel internationally. Thus, Morgan (2009), explicitly, and Oliver and Mätzke (2014), implicitly, reflect on the role of the OECD and European Union in promoting transnational policy learning. Nevertheless, as Lopreite and Macdonald's (2014) comparison of Argentina and Mexico suggests, national politics, played out in distinct institutional arenas, shape the way these travelling ideas are translated on the ground. Finally, Mätzke and Ostner (2010, p. 474) may mount the strongest argument linking ideas and path-shifting change. They declare that 'it is policy ideas that are crucial driving forces that turn political opportunities into political innovations'. In developing this argument, they distinguish between the different kinds of ideas (that is, paradigms, programs, frames and public sentiments) and link these to nationally distinct causal pathways (Mätzke and Ostner 2010, p. 475).

Transnational care chains

There is another new trend in care provision—care provided in the household by migrant women, especially (but not solely) for the frail elderly. This development is the product of the failure to address inequalities in care labour within the household (discussed above), inadequate state support for paid care provision in the household[5] in receiving countries, the latter's immigration policies and developments in the sending countries. As Hochschild (2000) has argued, this combination has resulted in the forging of 'global care chains' linking women in wealthy countries to women from poorer countries who provide care for their children or elderly parents, as well as to the others who fill the care gaps created in the sending country. As such, transnational care chains hold important implications for class and racial/ethnic as well as gender inequality.

More specifically, the (incomplete) transition to an earner–carer family norm and demographic developments (falling fertility, population ageing) have contributed to a 'care crisis' in wealthier countries while economic changes such as the elimination of jobs for those with less education and the rise in demand for high skills in the 'post-industrial' economy (Morel 2015) prod states to find ways to create jobs for those with less education and to enable highly educated women to work the long hours of their male counterparts. Esping-Andersen (1999) originally argued that universally accessible and publicly provided services of high quality helped these time-pressed post-industrial families while also providing decently paid, unionized jobs for care workers. However, states have also been under increasing pressure to find 'cost-effective' solutions to the care crisis, especially since the financial crisis of 2008. Home-based care thus appears attractive as it reduces the requirement to invest in developing care facilities and because the wages of (migrant) domestic care workers are low and frequently are not covered by national labour standards legislation.

Ideas have also played a part in promoting this development. Thus, neoliberalism and its celebration of the market have led to a greater emphasis on 'choice' and 'personalization'. This trend has also been fuelled by care receivers' advocates, especially by those representing persons with disabilities. In addition, certain place-specific 'ideals of care' (Kremer 2006) favour surrogate motherhood (Williams 2012) or the 'migrant in the family' (Bettio et al. 2006) over centre-based child care and residential elder care. These ideals appear more strongly rooted where the male breadwinner-female caregiver model was more firmly entrenched. Such ideals of care can in turn feed into racialized stereotypes regarding which migrants provide the 'best' care (Bettio et al. 2006, p. 276; Yeates 2012, p. 138).

Van Hooren (2012) suggests that the nature of a country's welfare regime influences the extent to which, and the way that, each country draws on migrant care workers. Thus, 'familialistic' welfare regimes such as those in Southern Europe tend to rely on the 'migrant in the family' especially to provide elder care while liberal regimes favour 'migrants in the market'. Demand for migrant domestic care workers is low in social democratic countries. The wealthy states also utilize a variety of instruments to subsidize paid domestic care, including cash for care schemes, vouchers, social contributions exemptions and tax rebates, and instrument choice is shaped by existing welfare or care regimes.

Williams (2012) argues that it is the interaction between care regimes, migration regimes and employment regimes that shapes national responses, including the choice of policy instruments. Thus, in the Southern European countries, Germany and Austria, migrant labour 'has been mainly home-based, whereas in those countries with more of a tradition of formal and institutionalized care, migrant workers are located in the expanding private markets in residential and nursing homes, and in home care agencies providing services to older people' (Williams 2012, p. 370). In Italy, which features a large informal sector and offers ex post regularizations to undocumented migrants, this combination has contributed to reliance on the migrant in the family for elder care. Migration regimes in turn help shape the sources of supply of migrant care workers. For instance, in addition to a quota especially set aside for migrant care workers, Spain allows Latin Americans to bring family members with them and also allows them to apply for Spanish citizenship after only two years of legal residence (Gorfinkel and Escrivá 2012, p. 131). Until recently, Canada had a 'live-in-caregiver' program that allowed migrant care workers to apply for citizenship after a certain period (Michel and Peng 2012).

Despite these differences, there is clearly a trend towards (1) instrument choice focused on demand rather than supply and (2) increased reliance on migrant care workers 'across sectors, sites and types of provision of care' (Williams 2012, p. 371). With regard to the first, demand side instruments deprive the state of the capacity to control the quality and location of supply (Morel 2015, p. 186). They also leave care workers in a vulnerable position, especially when the latter are migrants deprived of full citizenship rights. The second trend is also visible across the board, including in the Nordic countries that pioneered the social democratic model of publicly provided care services based on the universality principle. Thus, for instance, demand for 'au pairs' in Norway increased tenfold between 2000 and 2008 (Williams 2012, p. 369) and Denmark and Finland are among the major users of domestic service to provide elder care (Morel 2015). In 2007, Sweden's centre-right government introduced a tax break to encourage the expansion of domestic service, which has been used inter alia to provide elder care, and to a lesser extent, child care. Although these services account for a small part of child care provision in the Nordic countries, as we know from Streeck and Thelen (2005b), incremental modifications can amount to path-shifting change. Thus, as Morel (2015, p. 187) notes, in Denmark and Sweden

> not only has a private market for the wealthier elderly been created, it may also in the long run lead to incremental changes in the publicly financed sector as expectations vis-à-vis the public sector are lowered, but also as budget constraints become greater due to the lower fiscal revenues these schemes entail.

Thus far, we have focused on the receiving countries. What accounts for the flow of care workers from the sending countries? Certainly, the unemployment, poverty and informality fuelled by structural adjustment in the Global South and the 'transition' in Central and Eastern Europe have played an important role. Migration is also increasingly promoted as an important export by sending states, with the encouragement of the World Bank and donor agencies that tout remittances as a 'new' source of development assistance. For the care migrants themselves, although the wages are low by the standards of receiving countries and working conditions often degrading, the wages are still higher than those they can earn at home, even for skilled occupations such as nurses and teachers (Parreñas 2000; Bettio et al. 2006). More broadly, migration involves contradictory changes for women migrants.

> On the one hand there are role reversals, symbolized by women's decision to migrate and find employment abroad before men; likewise their new role in family maintenance takes place through the remittances sent. Both represent an increase in women's individual and financial autonomy, which can contribute to a process of 'undoing gender' . . . On the other hand, the prevalence and intensity of transnational mothering also implies a continuity of women's traditional roles; although subject to changes in time and space, there is evidence that migrant women's care of their children does not stop when they physically leave them. (Benería 2008, p. 10)

What of those left behind? As Lutz and Palenga-Möllenbeck (2012, p. 16) suggest, 'at the other end of this global care chain . . . are families in the sending countries, in particular children and elderly people in need of care, who pay the social and emotional cost of the deficit of care and emotional work'. At first glance, the departure of mothers/wives/daughters who leave to provide care in wealthier countries can be seen as a perverse form of defamilialization. The care gap thus created is rarely filled by states or markets, however. Thus, Martinez-Franzoni (2008, p. 87) argues that the welfare regimes of the main sending countries in Latin America are best understood as 'informal-familialist': they are 'unable to succeed in commodifying labour, while social protection and the formation of human capital are minimally decommodified'. As a result, the majority depend on extended and compound families for survival. More broadly, as Raghuram (2012, p. 164) argues, 'In many countries, the nuclear family may not be the norm and extended families may be commonplace . . . Many women may thus be involved in care distribution which means that the migration of one woman does not have as great an impact on care'. In other words, it is important not to assume that the nuclear family is the norm everywhere and that the children or elders left behind suffer from their mother's/daughter's absence.

Conclusion

In addition to contributing to new conceptions of agents and structures affecting the nature and extent of change (or continuity), the growing body of literature on policies that support the adult earner family offers several insights for welfare regime theory. In the first section, we discussed the importance of rethinking the defamilialization thesis, while in the second we reflected on current debates regarding the driving forces of change. In addition, there are some broader contributions we would like to signal.

First, building on insights from their research into movement away from the male breadwinner model even in states where, until very recently, it seemed deeply entrenched, Ferragina and Seeleib-Kaiser (2015) suggest a way analytically to capture various degrees of change by combining Hall's (1993) conception of first, second and third order change with a conception of regimes as 'spaces'. Thus, 'when we talk about liberal, Christian-democratic and social-democratic spaces we do not refer to specific countries but to *spaces* in which the 18 countries move over the period analyzed' (Ferragina and Seeleib-Kaiser 2015, p. 14, emphasis in the original). Esping-Andersen's (1999) regimes are configured as four quadrants: social democratic, liberal, Christian democratic and a fourth 'hybrid' regime. First order changes, such as a modest increase in generosity of paid leave programs, would not affect where a country was placed, but second order changes such as the introduction of new policy instruments or changes to how existing instruments are used could move a country from one quadrant closer to another or from the border of one quadrant into another. Third order change clearly involves a significant movement from one space/regime to another.

This conception would fit well with the insights Wincott (2006) has to offer. Presciently intervening in the current discussion of the difference between ideal types and real types, like Crouch and Keune (2005), Wincott recognizes that 'real types' of welfare states are normally 'heterogeneous and innovative hybridizations' and that this very complexity 'can provide an alternative range of inherited characteristics that can be drawn upon by reflexive social and political actors in developing opportunities for innovation . . .' (Wincott 2006, p. 302). Ellingsaeter's (2014) analysis of ongoing debates centred on daddy quotas and care allowances in the Nordic countries reflects precisely such fluidity and contradiction even in these pioneering countries. For Wincott (2006, p. 305), then, the concept of the welfare regime can usefully be supplemented by the notion of 'welfare settlement'—a complex pattern of public policy produced over time that leaves traces of subordinate ideas and admits internal tensions and contradictions (on 'welfare settlements'; see also Clarke and Newman 1997). This conception is in marked contrast to both the functionalist explanations offered by the Varieties of Capitalism approach and the treatment often accorded Esping-Andersen's regimes, as if the latter had a life of their own.

Finally, Blofield and Martinez-Franzoni (2015) offer a way of thinking about work-family typologies that would bring the growing domestic service sector, where migrant care workers are often concentrated, into the picture by including the regulation of labour standards of home-based care work. Their approach also would be useful in countries where there is a substantial informal sector. Thus, in addition to assessing the gender equality impact of leave ('sequential') programs and ('defamilializing') care services, they include an assessment of whether such policies contribute to social equity; that is, whether leaves or access to child care spaces are limited to those employed in the formal sector. While this approach seems especially important for analysing development in Southern Europe and the Global South, it is also increasingly relevant to the evaluation of North American and Western European regimes, given the expansion of precarious work there too.

NOTES

1 This also raises the question of the rights of those who provide extra-familial care, a point to be taken up below.

2 Some notable exceptions include Le Bihan and Martin (2006), Rostgaard and Szebehely (2012), Yeandle et al. (2012) and Armstrong et al. (2009).

3 As Saraceno and Keck (2010, p. 693) note, convergence in the area of care for small children has not been matched in the field of elder care.

4 Their definition differs substantially from, and can be seen as complementary to, that developed by social movement theorists like McAdam (1999), who were interested in assessing the ability of social forces to affect policy processes.

5 This excludes publicly financed and organized services such as the home help services that constituted an important part of Sweden's elder care system since these are unionized jobs and subject to labour standards legislation.

7   Social policy and the politics of diversity

As several scholars have noted (Banting 2008, p. 61; Sainsbury 2012, p. 21), less attention has been paid to the impact of ethnic/racial/ linguistic diversity in comparative social policy research, despite Williams's (1995) pioneering effort, which called for an approach to studying social policy regimes that integrated class, gender and 'race'/ ethnicity. Nearly a decade after the publication of her 'Race/ethnicity, gender, and class in welfare states: a framework for comparative analysis', however, new research began to appear, sparked in part by the growing importance of migration, especially, but not exclusively, that from South to North. We discussed the role of migrant labour in the provision of care in the previous chapter. In this chapter we focus on debates about the relationship between racial/ethnic diversity and social policy regimes. For Alesina and Glaeser (2004, 2008), the growing attention to migration in Europe raises the question of whether this would lead the welfare regimes of Western Europe to become less generous and more like that of the United States. For Banting (2008, pp. 59–60), migration and the related rise of multiculturalism raised two distinct questions: does ethnic/racial diversity in itself undermine the trust and solidarity that have underpinned the development of redistributive policies? And is solidarity in turn eroded by the multicultural policies enacted to accommodate newcomers?

To explore the complex relationship between diversity and social policy development, it is important to begin by looking back in time: has ethnic/racial/linguistic diversity impeded social policy development or is the US case unique? This chapter thus begins by looking at diversity and welfare state development in Western Europe, the Americas, and Australia and New Zealand. The second section focuses on contemporary issues of heterogeneity, recognition and redistribution and the way various authors have sought to unpack these. The third section turns to the broader connection between nationalism, including sub-state nationalism, and welfare state development. Some forms of nationalism create the kind of social solidarity that supports social policy expansion, whereas others support forms of social or territorial exclusion.

Is diversity an impediment to welfare state development?

The existence of deep racial divisions, compounded by ethnic diversity, has been used to help explain the limited scope of social policy in the United States, the paradigm exemplar of the residual liberal welfare regime (Esping-Andersen 1990). During the formative New Deal in the 1930s, the southern wing of the governing Democratic Party was able to use states' rights to facilitate the exclusion of southern blacks from welfare benefits (Quadagno 1988; Lieberman 1998). During the late 1950s, however, the civil rights movement launched a series of court cases that gave impoverished African American mothers access to the program. As a result of their success, 'between 1960 and 1967, the proportion of AFDC [Aid to Families with Dependent Children] recipients had shifted from 86 percent white to 46 percent white' (Levy and Michel 2002, p. 242), which in turn fuelled a move to get lone mothers off social assistance.[1] For the most part, however, the civil rights movement focused attention on addressing the civil and political rights of African Americans, rather than expanding their social rights (Quadagno 1994).

Alesina and Glaeser (2004, pp. 2–3) argue that the limited extent of the US welfare state reflects not only the political impact of racial/ethnic heterogeneity but also the existence of a political institutional complex that limits the role of the state. Of particular importance for the development of more generous welfare regimes in (continental) Western Europe, they suggest, was the introduction of electoral systems based on proportional representation, a reform championed by the European left and one that enabled it to influence social policy development. Here their argument accords with, and adds to, the power resource thesis discussed in Chapter 2. In other words, the introduction of proportional representation allowed the European left to have an impact even when it could only marshal a minority of votes.

Banting (2000) also highlights the importance of political institutions, not in terms of their impact on left-leaning parties but rather their capacity to mitigate the impact of diversity on welfare state development. Here the main difference is between the 'consociational democracies' of Belgium, Austria and the Netherlands and fragmented federal states like Canada, Switzerland and the United States. According to Banting (2000), the consociational model of decision making and collaboration among elites representing different class and religious subcultures enabled the former to build comprehensive welfare states despite religious, linguistic and other cultural divisions. In contrast, in Canada, Switzerland and the United States, federalism resulted in decentralized political institutions developed to manage ethno-linguistic diversity and, in the case of the United States, the distinction between the North and the slave-owning South. For instance, in Canada, federalism contributed to political contention centred on ethnic and regional differences, rather than class (Brodie and Jenson 1988), while the 'first-past-the-post' electoral system also made it more difficult for parties of the left to break through.

Banting's (2000) explanation for the development of generous social democratic welfare regimes in the Nordic countries highlights the combination of cultural homogeneity and centralized state structures. Brochmann (2015, p. 86), however, points out that such homogeneity is actually the result of policies pursued in the first half of the twentieth century, including 'a rather forceful intentional streamlining of the few existing ethnic minorities, notably in Sweden and Norway'. This involved the subordination of Sami culture to the dominant national narrative such that the Sami identify with their respective nation states (Burmeister Hicks and Somby 2005, pp. 275–6). A similar pattern occurred in the 'white settler states' of the Americas and Antipodes, albeit with important differences among them.

New Zealand, where the Maori account for 15 per cent of the population, is something of an outlier because the 1840 Treaty of Waitangi officially recognized Maori rights to political self-determination and the Maori electorate were granted seats in parliament in 1867 (Humpage 2010, p. 236). In addition, 'from the 1940s, welfare initiatives actively encouraged Maori to migrate from rural areas to meet the needs of capitalist production in the cities through relocation programmes (including access to state housing rentals) and redirection of economic assistance from rural to urban areas' (Humpage 2010, p. 243). In contrast, both the Australian and Canadian state, founded on the doctrine of 'terra nullis', officially denied prior inhabitation by indigenous peoples (Humpage 2010, p. 237; Tomiak 2011, Chapter 3). In both countries, indigenous peoples were only granted the right to vote in federal elections in the 1960s.[2] When Canada began to develop its welfare state at the end of World War II, however, indigenous peoples, including those living on reserves, were incorporated into universal programs like Family Allowances and Old Age Security (Shewell 2004, p. 238). The aim, however, was the same as those of the Swedish and Norwegian governments vis-à-vis the Sami population—to assimilate indigenous peoples into the dominant culture.[3] In Australia, indigenous peoples were only incorporated into income support legislation and collective bargaining systems in the 1960s (Humpage 2010, p. 237). Moreover, a system of shared responsibility agreements introduced in the 1990s 'required some communities to bargain for citizenship entitlements (such as education or health services) that other Australians take for granted' (Humpage 2010, p. 241).

In the above examples, the presence of indigenous peoples is not seen as having inhibited welfare state development, although their status was that of second class citizens. In Latin America, however, racial/ ethnic diversity, along with patterns of industrialization and political incorporation, may have contributed to uneven cross-national social policy development (Pribble 2011).[4] Overall, however, the evidence thus far suggests that other factors, including the structure of political institutions, have again played an important mediating role.

Growing diversity, demands for recognition and the future of welfare states

By the 1980s, Western European countries were beginning to recognize, albeit unevenly (Castles et al. 2006, chapter 2) that post-war 'temporary' workers had turned into permanent denizens, if not always citizens. Consciousness of the presence of these 'others' grew in the 1990s when the volume of migration increased, as did the variety of sources (increasingly drawn from outside the Western European core) and categories (increasing numbers of refugees, asylum seekers and undocumented migrants). In addition, although the traditional settler countries had long relied on immigration, in the latter part of the twentieth century they abandoned their 'Whiteness' bias and began to accept growing numbers of immigrants from across the globe. These changes were occurring as the crisis of Fordist production,[5] the post-industrial turn and the rise to prominence of neoliberal ideas were reshaping labour markets and putting pressure on existing welfare regimes. At the same time, however, growing international acknowledgement of the rights of immigrants and indigenous peoples combined with the rise of 'identity politics' to highlight demands of the newcomers—and indigenous peoples—for recognition. According to some, this gave rise to a potential 'redistribution–recognition' dilemma (Fraser 1997). In other words, this raised the question of whether demands for recognition ('multiculturalism') were undermining support for the welfare state.

The experience of two early adopters of multiculturalism—Canada (1971) and Sweden (1975)—suggests that recognition can in fact coincide with welfare state expansion.[6] Yet in both cases, these initiatives were taken before the major waves of non-Western immigration and the pressure to remodel welfare regimes along neoliberal lines. Have increased diversity and growing demands for its recognition contributed to the erosion of welfare regimes?

Banting and his colleagues (2006) tackled this question by identifying eight types of multicultural policies relevant to the recognition of immigrants[7] and using these to demarcate strong, modest and weak multicultural countries. A similar scale was constructed to measure public commitment to recognition of indigenous peoples' rights.[8] Both sets of measures were then correlated with welfare state change, measured in terms of social spending as a proportion of gross domestic product (GDP); redistribution effectiveness in reducing poverty and inequality; and the level of child poverty and the level of inequality (Banting et al. 2006, p. 64). They found 'no systematic pattern of countries that have adopted strong MCPs [multicultural policies] seeing an erosion in their welfare states relative to countries that have resisted such programmes'[9] (Banting et al. 2006, p. 83). Moreover, there was no correlation between changes in social spending and the size of immigrant populations (heterogeneity/redistribution tradeoff), although they found some evidence for this in countries 'with small but fast-growing foreign born populations' (Banting et al. 2006, p. 83).

This approach has insights to offer but, as Careja et al. (2015) argue, it is important to go beyond broad patterns of social expenditure to focus on programs that account for a disproportionate amount of immigrants' social benefits and to analyse eligibility criteria and conditions imposed on benefit claimants and their families. Ideally, the development of such an approach would also aim to integrate this set of issues into the wider literature on comparative welfare regimes. In an earlier article, Banting (2000) indeed suggested that the type of welfare regime does play an important part in determining whether immigrants (and indigenous peoples) are granted adequate support. Here, he suggested that the social democratic and corporatist regimes were better at integrating immigrants than liberal regimes like Australia's and Britain's, which require a substantial period of residence before immigrants can access old age pensions, disability or child support. Moreover, he noted that 'the largest savings [from the Clinton era] welfare reforms came not from restructuring AFDC but from restrictions on immigrant benefits' (Banting 2000, p. 24).

Sainsbury (2006, 2012) has explored this relationship further, arguing that such a study requires the simultaneous analysis of welfare regimes and incorporation regimes. The latter 'consist of rules and norms that govern immigrants' possibilities to become a citizen, to acquire permanent residence, and to participate in economic, cultural and political life' (Sainsbury, 2012, p. 6). Incorporation regimes thus include such things as consideration of a country's rules for citizenship acquisition, residence and work permits, and conditions for family reunification, as well as the whole gamut of rules governing different categories of immigrants. The rules governing an incorporation regime matter because they give rise to a system of stratification, articulated with but distinct from that associated with the welfare regime. For Sainsbury, incorporation regimes are simply classified as inclusive or exclusive, though

> countries that pursue inclusive immigrant policies do not necessarily have open and generous immigration policies. For example, Australia and Canada are often pointed to as countries with strong multicultural policies, but at the same time both countries employ an elaborate point system that excludes many immigrants, especially the poor and the uneducated. (2012, p. 16)

Sainsbury's important study examined two liberal (the UK and the US), two conservative (France and Germany) and two social democratic (Denmark and Sweden) welfare regimes, but showed that welfare regime type was no predictor of inclusiveness. In fact, while the US, France and Sweden have inclusive incorporation regimes, the UK, Germany and Denmark have restrictive regimes.

What role do ideas play in exacerbating or mitigating the impact of diversity on social policy development? Certainly, the way the policy problem is formulated matters. Thus, in both Australia and Canada, the problems faced by indigenous peoples have been framed by a mixture of social Darwinism and welfare dependency, which tends to weaken their rights (Humpage 2010, p. 242; Banting et al. 2013, p. 180). Tensions can also arise between the norms of the dominant culture and the way particular immigrant groups are represented. Thus, the (assassinated) Dutch politician, Pym Fortuyn's, anti-Islam rhetoric focused on the latter's (apparent) rejection of Dutch gender and sexual equality norms. A similar current runs through political discourses elsewhere in the North, especially but not exclusively articulated by right-wing populist parties. Gender equality norms are also used to marginalize certain immigrant groups, as reflected in debates on the Muslim veil.[10] Looking at the Danish case, Siim and Borchorst (2008, p. 10) argue that 'the achieved gender equality for women in "ethnic Danish families" is increasingly contrasted to a supposed patriarchal oppression of women in "migrant families"'. They go on to note that one of the carriers of this representation is the Danish People's Party, which has never been an advocate for gender equality.

The recent refugee crisis is Europe has provided fertile ground for the gendered framing of immigrants, in this case focused on young Muslim men arriving in mostly secular and 'gender-egalitarian' societies. Thus, in Germany the sexual violence ostensibly perpetrated by some asylum seekers in Cologne on New Year's Eve (31 December) 2015 was exploited by far-right activists and politicians. In response, the German government sponsored a sexual education website available in a dozen different languages and clearly directed at refugees, suggesting that 'unlike Germany, many countries don't teach sex education in schools, and many foreigners, including many of the refugees, come from states where sex is a taboo topic' (Breitenbach 2016). Using graphic images depicting interracial couples in various sexual positions, this website exacerbated the ongoing and sometimes nasty debate about whether immigrants from the Middle East and North Africa can adapt to life in countries like Germany (Breitenbach 2016). More generally, the refugee crisis has been conflated with terrorist incidents by the far right to bolster its claims that Muslim immigrants cannot adapt to Western societies and thus pose a threat to national identity. In the 2016 American presidential primaries, Donald Trump's suggestion that Muslims be banned from entering that country reflected the rise of xenophobic nationalism in many Northern countries.

Nationalism and social policy

The above discussion raises the important yet understudied issue of the relationship between nationalism and social policy, which can take a number of distinct forms (Béland and Lecours 2012). First, majority nationalism is the collective identity 'projected by the central . . . state' (Lecours and Nootens 2011, p. 4). In many countries, this type of nationalism has historically been fostered by realities like colonialism, military conflicts and the creation of national public education systems (Lecours and Nootens 2011). Although less visible than forms of nationalism that challenge the existence of the central state, majority nationalism is not only about low-intensity expressions of national pride; under certain circumstances, this type of nationalism can feed far-right political movements that seek to redefine the nation in a way that excludes outsiders. The rise of far-right, anti-immigration parties like the Danish People's Party,and France's Front National are prime expressions of far-right majority nationalism (Wodak et al. 2013).

At the same time, it is important to recognize that by no means all forms of national pride lead to far-right xenophobia. In fact, in a country like Canada, multiculturalism has become a permanent feature of the national identity articulated by the central state. Yet even there, key aspects of multiculturalism have become controversial in recent years, for example, when a woman's right to wear the niqab at citizenship ceremonies became an issue in the 2015 federal election campaign. Moreover, in a number of countries, the recent influx of African and Middle Eastern refugees, coupled with fears stemming from global terrorism, has exacerbated debate about Islam and the status of Islam in Western societies. These debates have been exploited by far-right politicians like Donald Trump, who spread Islamophobic fears to gain political support from older, less educated, white voters (Saunders 2015).

One way majority nationalism connects with social policy concerns the issue of 'welfare chauvinism', a concept that refers to the ongoing push to exclude perceived 'outsiders' from national health and social benefits. For instance, in the United Kingdom, the UK Independence Party (UKIP) wants to limit 'access to the National Health Service to legal residents of Britain' (Edsall 2014). This is only one example of a broad push to exclude at least some categories of immigrants from welfare state programs in advanced industrial countries. According to van der Waal et al. (2013), welfare chauvinism is more prevalent in conservative and liberal than in social democratic welfare regimes. Nevertheless, as noted above, welfare chauvinism can also arise in social democratic countries like Denmark.

Second, sub-state nationalism refers to the affirmation of a political and territorial identity as distinct from that of the central state. As Banting (2000, p. 14) argues, 'the challenge to social citizenship posed by the politics of international migration seems less compelling when compared with the politics of contending nationalisms, where the conception of the political community within which redistribution should take place is contested much more directly and powerfully'. This challenge to the central state occurs when a country includes at least one group that identifies primarily with a nation other than the one projected by the central state (Béland and Lecours 2012). Examples of sub-state nationalism include Catalonia and the Basque Country (Spain), Flanders (Belgium), Quebec (Canada) and Scotland and Wales (United Kingdom). Although sub-state nationalist parties like the Parti Québécois and the Scottish National Party make cultural and identity claims to justify the push for greater autonomy or outright independence from the central state, nationalist demands can intersect directly with welfare state issues.

For instance, nationalists have long articulated a discourse about how independence, or greater devolution, would foster the advent of more progressive social policy in Scotland. Conversely, in Belgium, Flemish nationalists have criticized the flow of fiscal resources and social benefits towards Wallonia, a poorer, French-speaking region located in the south of the country. These two examples suggest that sub-state nationalism can either have expansive or conservative implications for social policy (Béland and Lecours 2012). Finally, social programs operated by the central state can offset the centripetal forces associated with sub-state nationalism by fostering a sense of country-wide citizenship and national unity. This is especially true in culturally and ethnically fragmented countries such as Canada and the United Kingdom, where post-World War II welfare state expansion triggered the advent of universal social citizenship consistent with the national unity project of the central state (Banting 2005; McEwen 2006).

A similar logic guided social policy development in sub-Saharan Africa immediately after independence when political leaders of newly independent states such as Ghana emphasized the need for free public education and health care to bring people of various ethnic backgrounds together (Kpessa et al. 2011). Although many of these policies were later dismantled in the context of structural adjustment programs, their very existence suggests that, as in developed multinational countries such as Canada and the United Kingdom, social programs can play a positive national unity role in ethnically diverse societies such as the ones found in post-colonial Africa.

This discussion of the relationship between national unity and social policy should not obscure the fact that, across the world, decentralization has become a major issue in social policy reform. To be sure, federal states have long allocated a greater social policy role to subnational units,[11] albeit to different degrees (Obinger et al. 2005) and even in the 'unitary' Nordic states local governments have maintained they were 'responsible for a wide range of functions in the fields of education, housing, health and hospital care' (Fargion 2000, p. 64) even before they assumed a critical role in the provision of social care services. More recently, the European Union's endorsement of the principle of subsidiarity has helped to legitimize the regionalization of social programming in key policy areas (Spiker 1991). Although decentralization can help adapt social policy benefits and delivery to local contexts, there is always a risk it can erode social citizenship, understood in terms of uniformity of social rights within national boundaries. Striking a balance between the responsiveness to local needs and the enduring quest for territorial integration represents an ongoing challenge for contemporary social policy. Thus, in addition to examining how states deal with ethnic and racial diversity, it is also important to probe the way they try to come to terms with local and territorial diversity while preserving common principles in designing social policies.

Conclusion

As this chapter suggests, the complex relationship between the growing diversity of populations, representations of diversity and (political and social) institutions is an important one to unpack. Scholars like Banting (2008) and Sainsbury (2012) have helped lay the foundations for such work but more is needed, especially as the horizons expand to include social policy development across the globe. There is also a need for more research on the relationship between nationalism and social policy that focuses on both majority and sub-state nationalism. Regarding sub-state nationalism, the case of Scotland in the aftermath of the June 2016 'Brexit' vote is particularly fascinating as it connects direct sub-state nationalism with continental integration. Finally, although most of the research about immigration, nationalism and social policy currently deals with advanced industrial countries, these issues are just as important in the Global South, especially in post-colonial, multi-ethnic countries such as India and Nigeria that struggle with massive diversity and fragmentation.

NOTES

1 See Lister et al. (2007, pp. 94–100) and the special issue of *Social Politics* co-edited by Kilic et al. (2008).

2 Although indigenous soldiers returning from World War II were allowed to vote in Canadian federal elections if they renounced their status, few did. The right to vote was officially extended in 1960. In Australia, returning soldiers and those who had acquired the right to vote at the (sub-) state level (that is, not in Queensland or Western Australia) could vote as of 1949, but the latter restriction was only removed in 1962. And until 1967, Aborigines were not counted as part of the Australian population.

3 Other methods of assimilation were more intrusive, most notably the residential schools in place for much of the twentieth century, and later, the removal of Aboriginal children from homes 'judged by European middle class standards to be inappropriate'. The children were then 'placed in institutional care or adopted out to European families deemed to meet such standards' (Finkel 2006, p. 316).

4 On racial hierarchies and citizenship in Latin America, see Rojas (2002) and Wade (2004).

5 Fordist production refers not simply to the advent of the assembly line but to the larger system of mass production that played such a central part in the post-war boom in OECD countries. The Keynesian welfare state constituted an important complement to the extent that it supported mass consumption, that is, people's ability to purchase these mass produced goods.

6 Canada officially adopted a bilingual, multicultural identity in the second major period of social policy expansion (Myles and St Arnaud 2006, p. 345) while Sweden's embrace of multiculturalism coincided with renovation of its welfare regime to incorporate gender equality.

7 These are: constitutional, legislative or parliamentary affirmation of multiculturalism; the adoption of multiculturalism in school curricula; inclusion of ethnic representation/sensitivity in the mandate of public media or media licensing; exemptions from dress codes and Sunday closings; dual citizenship; funding of ethnic group organizations; funding of bilingual or mother-tongue instruction; and affirmative action for disadvantaged immigrant groups (Banting et al. 2006, pp. 56–7).

8 These are: the recognition of land, self-government and cultural rights; the recognition of customary law; guarantees of representation/consultation and upholding/signing treaties; constitutional or legislative affirmation of the distinct status of indigenous peoples; support for international instruments on indigenous rights; and affirmative action (Banting et al. 2006, p. 62).

9 Their study focuses on the traditional welfare states of the North. Had they looked to Latin America, however, they may have found a positive correlation between recognition of indigenous rights and welfare state expansion in the wake of the 'pink wave' of left victories. As van Cott (2006, p. 272) argues, 'multicultural movements have articulated a new discourse that links ethnic and economic claims and in so doing, have revitalized low-income/leftist reform coalitions'.

10 Full of racial and gendered overtones and targeting lone mothers, especially African American ones, this anti-welfare campaign culminated in the enactment of the conservative 1996 welfare reform (Mink 1998).

11 The issue of the impact of federalism on welfare state development has received limited attention. In addition to the Obinger et al. (2005) volume, see Pierson (1995). On the impact of federal architectures on measures to reconcile work and family life, see Mahon and Brennan (2013).

8 Globalization and social policy

Globalization was initially seen as a threat to the welfare state. It was believed that the economic pressures generated by neoliberal globalization would inexorably lead to welfare state retrenchment or its dissolution and replacement by a lean 'competition' state (Cerny 1997). Yet the global rediscovery of poverty (Noël 2006), the challenges to territorially based conceptions of social rights posed by the increasing flow of migrants, not to mention the enhanced transnational spread of policy ideas and definitions of 'best practice', have put social policy issues on the global agenda. With the publication of *Global Social Policy: International Organisations and the Future of Welfare* (Deacon et al. 1997), a new concept—that of global social policy—and a new terrain of research opened up, pushing researchers beyond the methodological nationalism of traditional comparative social policy to incorporate transnational forces and agencies.

This chapter begins with a brief reprise of earlier debates about the impact of economic globalization on welfare states of the North. While that debate appeared to have been won by those who contested the retrenchment thesis in various ways, the shock waves unleashed by the 2008 financial crisis rekindled the debate between those arguing that the global crisis reinforced austerity politics at the national scale and those asserting that welfare state 'recalibration' remains very much on the agenda. The second section reflects on the idea of global social policy, the main actors involved in shaping it and the parameters of what Deacon (2007) called the global 'war of position' between those advocating neoliberal reforms and those pushing for the social rights of all. The final section turns to various efforts to overcome currently fragmented governance structures and simultaneous attempts to counter the hegemony of the international financial institutions (IFIs), notably the World Bank and the International Monetary Fund (IMF), over the rights-based organs of the United Nations (UN).

Globalization, crisis and the end of the welfare state?

The initial debate about the consequences of globalization pitted those who argued that pressures generated by neoliberal globalization would lead to a 'race to the bottom' (Mishra 1999) against those who countered that states with more developed welfare regimes were better placed to cushion the impact of increased international competition (Garrett 1998; Swank 2002). Pierson (1998), however, helped to shift the debate by pointing out that internal structural changes associated with the transition from industrial to post-industrial socio-economic structures are at least as important as globalization. More importantly, although

> these transitions create an environment of ongoing austerity . . . the strength of support for public social provision in most countries makes the dismantling of the welfare state highly unlikely. Instead, successful reform is likely to be based on compromise and to take the form of *restructuring and modernization of the social contract*. (Pierson 1998, p. 539, emphasis added)

Accordingly, research turned to focus on efforts to modernize the welfare state, calling upon social policy concepts discussed in Chapter 5. Thus, for some it meant identifying appropriate measures to deal with the 'new social risks', while for others it involved charting the emergence of a social investment perspective potentially offering a post-neoliberal conception of social policy.

The 2008 financial crisis—or crises as Farnsworth and Irving (2015) argue—brought back the spectre of globalization-induced austerity as the damage quickly spread beyond the burst US housing market bubble, leading to bank failures in the UK, Ireland and Iceland.[1] The 'Great Recession' of 2009 then spread throughout the Eurozone, as well as the export-oriented Asian economies of China and Japan, while the 2009 European sovereign debt crisis hit the Portuguese, Spanish, Italian and Irish economies with particular severity.

In addition to the internationalization of financial markets, McBride (2015, p. 34) argues that international institutions have contributed to the 'locking-in' of neoliberal 'fiscal consolidation' with negative implications for social programs. Thus, inter- and supranational institutions—the 'troika' of the European Commission, the Central European Bank and the IMF—have played a direct role in the restructuring of social programs in Southern European countries (Ayhan and McBride

2015; León et al. 2015). As Guillén and Pavolini (2015, p. 148) argue, the vulnerability of Southern European countries was 'partially related to internal structural rigidities and problems (especially Greece, Portugal and Italy), partially as an outcome of global financial crisis and the burst of the bubble (Spain)'. The reform packages negotiated at a distance from national parliaments and other organs of popular representation imposed a marked retrenchment of social rights and, at best, a process of 'subtractive recalibration' that reduced the difference between 'insiders' and 'outsiders' largely by reducing protections previously afforded the former (Guillén and Pavolini 2015, p. 150). In Spain, a reform process that had begun to address the 'new social risks' came to a halt (Guillén and Pavolini 2015, p. 150). Progress in reforming social policies in the name of gender equality has also slowed (Leschke and Jepsen 2014) in other European countries. Yet austerity has not become 'the only game in Europe', as van Kersbergen et al.'s (2014) comparison of British, Danish, Dutch and German social policy reforms in the wake of the crisis suggests. The timing, scope and scale of the impact of international forces continue to be shaped by national circumstance, including national politics (Farnsworth and Irving 2015).

Canada, the UK and (later) Australia are among the countries that 'chose' austerity rather than having it imposed by international constraints. In contrast, under the Obama administration the US was able to pursue 'social policy expansion through stealth' in some areas, notably the substantial enrichments related to unemployment insurance (Boychuk 2015). In China, too, the crisis has, if anything, accelerated the process of social policy expansion (Hong and Kongshøj 2014; Cook and Lam 2015). Social policy expansion was also occurring in other major Asian countries and in other parts of the Global South, particularly in other 'emerging' countries in Latin America and southern Africa. In many respects, these reforms can be seen as a response to earlier crises. Thus, Peng (2011, p. 69) links Japan's and Korea's social policy reform wave to the opening created by the 1997 Asian financial crisis. The same crisis opened the way for ongoing efforts to develop a social policy infrastructure in Indonesia (Sumarto et al. 2010; Peck and Theodore 2015, pp. 115–18). Similarly, the 1994 peso crisis provided the context for the development of Mexico's conditional cash transfer (CCT) program, PROGRESA/Oportunidades (Peck and Theodore 2015, p. 65), just as the 2001 Argentinean crisis inaugurated important social policy developments by the centre-left Kirchner government.

While crises stemming from international economic shocks often provided the immediate impetus for these reforms, in some cases (for example, Korea) they simply accelerated processes already underway. In other cases, however, reform took time and experimentation to unfold (Starke et al. 2013). As Pierson's (2011) comparative analysis of social policy since the 1970s cautions, a final assessment of the 'permanent austerity vs. social innovation' debate can only be made over the *longue durée*. Nevertheless, it is clear that national solutions to the challenges posed by the economic crisis are not worked out in a vacuum. Global actors are increasingly involved in helping to shape the definition of social policy issues and the range of possible solutions. Moreover, neoliberal orthodoxy is being challenged on several fronts. As Whiteside (2015, p. 258) argues,

> macroeconomic researchers are increasingly reporting not only on the lack of short-run benefits but also that fiscal consolidation is stunting longer-term prospects for economic recovery; 'New Keynesian' thinking is growing in prominence in academic and popular press circles, guided by influential economists such as Paul Krugman; and equally influential policy advisers within leading international organizations and institutions . . . have begun to openly question the use of austerity.

In social policy terms, social investment, particularly the social democratic version, continues to promise an alternative to permanent austerity.

Global social policy

The publication of *Global Social Policy: International Organisations and the Future of Welfare* (1997) helped to establish global social policy as an emerging field of research. To be sure, those working on development had long recognized the policy influence of international organizations, but it was the involvement of international actors in shaping the post-Soviet transition that prompted Deacon and his colleagues to reflect on growing transnational attention to and involvement in social issues (Yeates 2008, p. 11). For Deacon (2007, p. 1), global social policy 'consists of two things: first it is the social policy prescriptions for national social policy being articulated by global actors such as international organisations; second, it is the emerging supranational social policies and mechanisms of global redistribution, global social regulation and global social rights'. We shall discuss the latter in the next section. In this section, the focus is on the former.

Global actors may be involved in developing and promoting social policy ideas through international conferences that identify pressing problems and ways of solving these, the development of indicators to monitor and compare national performance and the provision of technical assistance, as well as through more coercive measures such as the attachment of conditions to financial support. Whatever the mechanism, some policy ideas travel more readily than others. Von Gliszczynski and Leisering (2016, p. 5) highlight five factors that facilitate diffusion:

1. An international organization defines the idea—or 'model'—as part of its mandate.
2. It 'takes up earlier models, either models proposed by international organizations or models already adopted in some states, rather than defining a new model from scratch'.
3. It gains legitimacy through reference to 'theories and/or empirical evidence provided by experts from selected expert communities and other organizations considered as peers'.
4. 'The model is framed by more general ideas from higher layers of knowledge . . . and the model is linked to strong ideas from policy fields other than social policy'.
5. Finally, 'the model is given a name that appeals to a global public . . . and discursive practices are used to underpin the model, such as narratives and quantitative evidence'.[2]

Yet more is involved than this. As Jenson (2010) emphasizes, the creation of 'political space' is crucial for the diffusion of policy ideas. Thus, while neoliberal ideas came to the fore in the 1980s, they have not been uncontested. In fact, Deacon (2007, p. 16) went so far as to suggest that

> powerful states (notably the USA), powerful organisations (such as the IMF) and even powerful disciplines (such as economics) contend with other powerful states (notably the EU, China and Brazil), other powerful organisations (such as the ILO) and other disciplines (such as social and political science) to engage in a war of position[3] regarding the content of global policy.

For Deacon, the battle over global social policy has come to centre on the contest between a neoliberal emphasis on 'safety nets' for the very poor versus universal policies that include the middle class.[4] The latter is seen as both ethically and politically important, following the logic of the 'paradox of redistribution' discussed in Chapter 3. Thus, since the 'rediscovery' of poverty in the 1990s, the World Bank has advocated a residual approach to social spending while the Organisation for Economic Co-operation and Development (OECD) has championed a social investment perspective (Jenson 2010). This division is also very clear in the field of policies for early childhood (Mahon 2016). Perhaps more surprisingly, it arises in the debate over CCTs, which have been championed by the World Bank as a social investment policy targeting the poor. As Peck and Theodore (2015, p. 129) argue, however, 'one of the more perverse consequences of the CCT "avalanche" may have been to keep open, even to animate, a contra-conditionalities position on the moving terrain of social protection policy'.

More importantly, Peck and Theodore's (2015, p. 120) analysis underscores a critical feature of the 'diffusion' process:

> Social policy dialogues may have been transnationalized to a significant degree, and they may often be conducted under the long shadow cast by favored global models, but at the same time they are inescapably demarcated and animated by domestic political pressures, discursive representations of 'the problem,' and policy precedents. The experimental field that has been established around CCTs is a multi-actor space, and just as favored models come and go, so also does the editing of the approved policy-making script tend to become a continuous process.

In other words, policy ideas do not 'diffuse' smoothly across the globe, nor is the flow unidirectional, emanating from powerful international organizations and/or states (see also Kingfisher 2013 and Clarke et al. 2015). Rather the flow is multi-directional—from South to North and South to South and from national (and sub-national) to global, as well as from international organizations (IOs) to nation states. Along the way, the ideas themselves are transformed. As Tsing (2005, p. 6) argues, such travel is not 'friction-free'. Rather, the flow is characterized by friction and while 'friction makes global connections powerful and effective . . . without even trying, friction gets in the way of the smooth operation of global power. Difference can disrupt, causing everyday malfunctions as well as unexpected cataclysms'.

It is important also to recognize that even international organizations like the World Bank are neither monolithic nor static. The Bank's campaign to promote privatization of pensions nicely illustrates these multiple 'complications'. The movement originated in Pinochet's Chile during the early 1980s, led by a team of Chilean economists trained in the 'Chicago school' of neoliberal economics (Orenstein 2005, p. 190). These ideas were picked up by the World Bank nearly a decade later, under the leadership of then Chief Economist Larry Summers. This position was contested from outside by the ILO, which argued 'that there is no demographic imperative leading to privatisation, that the European-type schemes are reformable and sustainable, and that the privatisation strategy is merely a cover to increase the share of private capital savings' (Deacon 2007, p. 65). It was also contested from the inside. Thus, while *Averting the Old Age Crisis* (World Bank, 1994), produced by the 'California Girls' (Estelle James and her colleagues) in the World Bank's Development Economics section, laid out the case for privatization, the operations division for Eastern Europe was producing a document 'more in keeping with existing practice in Eastern Europe' (Deacon 2007, p. 33). Under the guidance of the Head of Social Protection, Robert Holzmann, the Bank invested 'considerable resources in convincing government civil servants of the wisdom of adopting the multi-pillar approach' (Deacon 2007, p. 34). In 1999, however, Summers's successor, Joseph Stiglitz, launched a powerful critique of pension privatization. Although Stiglitz's removal in 1999 left Holzmann free to push his neoliberal reforms, which he did with considerable (but still uneven)[5] success, in 2005 and 2006 the Bank went on to publish two reports 'that produced a damning critique of pension privatization and World Bank advocacy of it' (Béland and Orenstein 2013, p. 130). With Holzmann's retirement and his replacement by 'a labor market expert with limited interest in pension privatization' (Béland and Orenstein 2013, p. 131), the Bank quietly dropped this element of neoliberal orthodoxy.

These shifts in the Bank's position did not, of course, occur in a vacuum; they were reinforced by events in Chile and the United States. Thus, around the same time as the Bank dropped its campaign for privatized pensions, the then newly elected centre-left Chilean government launched a critique of privatization as part of its broader poverty reduction campaign. In the United States, the Bush government failed to push through privatization of its old age Social Security system (Béland and Orenstein 2013, pp. 131–3). In other words, the outcome of the battle of ideas within and between institutions is influenced by 'real world' events.

While much of the attention has focused on international organizations, Yeates (2008, p. 13) has convincingly argued for broadening the range of actors to include inter alia 'the activities of non-elites ... notably social movement and non-governmental organisations operating in the numerous shadow congresses and social fora that accompany international governmental meetings'. Such a move helps shed light on the critical role played by an international non-governmental organization (NGO), HelpAge International, in the diffusion of social pensions—that is, flat rate pensions financed out of general revenue, designed to include those in the informal economy not covered by existing social insurance programs—albeit with support from the ILO and the (post-privatization) World Bank (von Gliszczynski and Leisering 2016, p. 8; see also Walker-Bourne et al. 2011). Boris and Fish (2014) have documented Household Workers Worldwide's successful campaign to get the ILO to champion the rights of domestic workers. Deacon (2008, Chapter 5) also argues for the inclusion of think tanks, epistemic communities, consulting companies and, of course, transnational business groups.[6]

Broadening the scope of actors to include social movements, transnational advocacy networks (Keck and Sikkink 1999) and/or 'alter-globalization' sites such as the World Social Forum (Pleyers 2011; Conway 2012; Friesen 2012) also has the potential to expand the parameters of Deacon's (2007) original 'war of position' to include discourses on gender equality that transcend the liberal versions favoured by IOs (Marx Ferree and Tripp 2006; Dufour et al. 2010); conceptions of 'alternative regionalisms' to those enshrined in liberalizing trade agreements (Olivier and Brennan 2010); notions of transnational citizenship rights for migrants (Sarvasy and Longo 2004); and radical green scenarios such as 'de-growth' (Dimaria et al. 2013).

Transnational social governance

As Deacon (2007) noted, global social policy also refers to transnational social policies, the thin but growing layer of global rights (women's rights, indigenous rights, migrants' rights) that burgeoned especially in the 1990s, aided by a series of UN conferences and world summits, global regulations such as ILO covenants, and redistribution programs meant to deal with poverty and inequality on a global scale. Existing governance structures that are designed to support such global social policies, however, are fragmented. As Deacon (2007, p. 10) notes, 'at present the world has in effect two global ministries of health, two global ministries of education and two global ministries of social protection'.[7] In addition, 'because of the lack of a single, coherent, global government, global policies normally require cooperation from state organizations at the national or local level to be implemented' (Orenstein 2005, p. 177). In fact, the absence of hierarchy underlines the multi-scalar nature of transnational social governance (Keil and Mahon 2009).

One of the key issues, as suggested by Deacon's (2007) 'two ministries' thesis, has been the push by rights-oriented UN agencies and their allies to secure, if not hegemony, at least substantial influence over the more powerful IFIs. The Millennium Development Goals (MDGs) offer one such example. The UN conferences and world summits, culminating in the 1995 World Summit for Social Development in Copenhagen, provided the impetus behind these, but it was the OECD's Development Advisory Committee (DAC) that seized the initiative, boiling the results of these conferences down to six international goals (DAC 1996). These goals were picked up and elaborated into the MDGs through the initiative of then UN Secretary General, Kofi Annan, with the support of the World Bank, which had by that time embraced a poverty reduction agenda. As Fukuda-Parr and Hulme (2011, p. 22) note, the broad aims of the original Millennium Development Declaration were then reduced to 18 targets and 48 indicators by a smaller interagency group of technocrats largely drawn from the DAC, the World Bank and the United Nations Development Programme (UNDP). Yet, although the MDGs did identify one indicator of inequality, set global targets with a clear timeline for meeting these and included the development of a 'global partnership', they can be regarded as a 'retreat from the more universalism formulations of the Copenhagen social summit' (Deacon 2013) because they are centred on the neoliberal social policy of targeting the poorest of the poor. They also had a limited goal in terms of universal public service provision in the fields of primary education and reproductive health (Deacon 2007, p. 61).[8] The Sustainable Development Goals that succeeded the MDGs go farther than the latter, by for example putting equality in a more central position and substantially expanding the indicators related to gender equality.

The global social protection floor represents a bolder initiative, one in which the ILO and its allies have played a critical role. In substantive terms, the 'floor' sought to establish a global commitment to basic social protection guarantees, especially in the areas of access to health care and income security, across the life cycle. More importantly from the standpoint of global social governance, the ILO and its allies sought to establish a multi-scalar governance structure that would bring the IFIs around to endorsing the principle of universality.

Like the MDGs, this initiative has its roots in the 1990s, notably the Social Development Summit chaired by Juan Somavía, who went on to become the director general of the ILO; the annual seminars convened by the Globalism and Social Policy Programme (GASPP) from 1997 to 2004; and the work of the OECD-DAC's Poverty Network (POV-NET) among others (Deacon 2013, p. 19). Within the ILO, the impetus for transcending the organization's focus on Bismarckian social insurance programs and formal sector workers came from both the Social Policy and Development unit and from Guy Standing's InFocus Programme on Socio-Economic Security (Deacon 2013, Chapter 2 passim). The ILO-initiated 2004 World Commission on the Social Dimensions of Globalisation first issued the call for a global social floor, but it was the meeting on financial social policy in a globalizing world, held in Kellokoski, Finland, where the ILO began to enlist the support of other UN agencies, major donor agencies and international NGOs like HelpAge International and Save the Children, a partnership formalized in 2007.

The case for a floor was given added impetus by the successful social pensions and CCT experiments. As the then-head of the ILO section on financing social protection, Michael Cichon, would later remark, 'The demonstration that a basic set of social security benefits is affordable, also for developing countries, first broke the spell that had beset the social security development debate [but] it took a global financial and economic crisis to push social security to the top of the international agenda' (cited in Peck and Theodore 2015, p. 125). More specifically, the UN was eager to regain the initiative from the IFIs as chief manager of the responses to the 2008 financial crisis, and Somavía was able to use his position as chair of the high-level panel on programs for UN System Chief Executive Board to make the floor a key part of the UN's response. The UN Social Protection Floor Initiative board initially charged with the task of coordinating initiatives set to work developing a Manual and Strategic Framework for joint UN-country operations. More importantly, it laid out a multi-scalar architecture for implementing the floors. As the Bachelet report, prepared for the 2012 G20 meeting noted, social protection floor activities at the country level are [to be] coordinated and executed through a national Social Protection Floor Task Force led by governments and composed of the social partners, social security institutions, NGOs, donors, bilateral agencies as well as the UN Social Protection Floor country team that draws on country, regional and headquarters staff of the operating UN agencies and Bretton Woods institutions. (ILO 2011, p. 76)

The UN Resident Coordinator was to play a key role in launching the floor process at the country level, organizing the UN Social Protection Floor country team and seeking the creation of a national Task Force.

To be successful, however, the initiative needed the support of the IFIs, as well as major donors. Here, the World Bank's 2012 adoption of a new social policy orientation helped it to look more favourably on the initiative, and perhaps to gain control over it. Thus, the Bank's support came at the price of the establishment of a new governing body, the Social Protection Inter Agency Cooperation Board (SPIAC-B,) which would be co-chaired by the ILO and the Bank. As Deacon (2014) notes, the two agencies continue to be divided on a host of substantive and methodological issues and it is by no means clear whether the ILO and its allies will be able to triumph. More importantly, although there had been some rapprochement between the ILO and the IMF, it is not clear whether the latter's 'advice' will help to create the fiscal space needed to implement the reforms, especially as the latter seems to have stepped back from its social policy concern (Vetterlein 2015).

In addition to these efforts on the global scale, there has been growing interest in regional initiatives. These have been fuelled by questioning

a Northern-driven reformed globalization strategy imposing 'inappropriate' . . . global social and labour standards . . . For some in the Global South . . . the point is not so much to reform and strengthen extant 'global' institutions that are controlled by and operate in the interests of the North, but to . . . outflank them by creating new countervailing . . . sources of power properly serving the interests of the Global South. (Yeates and Deacon 2010, p. 28)

Deacon and Macovei (2010) identify three types of international organizations operative at a regional scale: the regional development banks; regional offices of UN social agencies like the United Nations

Children's Emergency Fund (UNICEF); and the regional economic commissions of the UN, such as the Economic Commission for Latin America and the Caribbean (ECLAC). These are active in promoting transnational social policy governance within their regions, primarily around issues such as the management of labour migration, working towards social security transferability within the region and monitoring communicable diseases. The UN social agencies and regional commissions have also been active in promoting social dialogue mechanisms and best practice learning.[9]

There are also initiatives to promote 'alternative regionalism', that is, projects that seek to develop alternatives to neoliberal globalization at the regional scale. Olivier and Brennan (2010) studied four of these: the Hemispheric Social Alliance (Latin America), the Southern African Peoples' Solidarity Network, the ASEAN Civil Society Conference and Solidarity for Asian Peoples Advocacy. All four rejected the privatization of essential public services and sought to advance policies that address basic needs (Olivier and Brennan 2010, p. 76). They called for regional mechanisms to defend workers' rights to decent work, including migrants' rights. In recognition of the links between the economic and social spheres, they also called for regional regulation of financial markets and the operations of transnational corporations, and the establishment of new forms of solidaristic financing within the region (Olivier and Brennan 2010). There is also a movement for 'Another Europe'. The Peoples Agenda for Alternative Regionalisms (PAAR) additonally promotes cooperation among the various alt-regionalism projects.[10]

Little work has been done focusing on sub-national units. Yet sub-national experiments with CCTs in Brazil had an impact not only on national policy but also caught the attention of the World Bank (Peck and Theodore 2015). Even less attention has been paid to the role of 'global cities' in transnational social governance. Hudson (2012, pp. 458–9) has been one of the few who has called for the analysis of these cities' social policy implications, arguing that such analysis

> will help us better understand the impact of macro-level pressures on policy makers (i.e. globalization) as articulated through micro-level actors (i.e. individuals working in key global organizations located in global cities) operating in key meso-level institutions (e.g. multinational corporations) and interacting with other meso-level institutions (e.g. policy networks, political institutions).

As he notes, such sites typically have more diverse populations with a greater share of migrants, are characterized by higher levels of social and economic inequality and, at the same time, are linked into transnational networks of various kinds. In fact, cities like New York, Paris and Geneva are where key international organizations are headquartered and often act as centres for the operation of transnational social movements. They can also act as incubators for important social policy innovations such as the 'living wage' movement or even experiments with basic income programs.

Conclusion

While the original fears that globalization would lead to the withering away of the welfare state proved alarmist, the 2008 financial crisis and its continuing reverberations across the globe served to rekindle the debate. At the same time, even while the Southern European countries were being driven to adopt severe austerity budgets, important social policy experiments were unfolding in parts of the Global South. Moreover, the crisis provided an opening for the ILO and its allies to launch the global social protection floor initiative, which aimed not only to promote the adoption of basic universal social programs in the South but also to establish a global governance architecture that would bring the IFIs on board with their social agenda. Nevertheless, global social governance remains a messy business. It is too early to assess the fate of the global social protection floor initiative, much less the Sustainable Development Goals adopted in the fall of 2015 as successors to the MDGs. Regional organizations and networks do not simply function as conduits for 'global' initiatives, but are also sites of attempts at social regulation and redistribution. In the future, perhaps, more attention will be paid to the role played by global cities. Thus, as Yeates (2014, p. 35) notes, there is 'not one single global social policy but many and contested versions of global social policy circulate within the multi-faceted, multilayered, and incoherent set of institutions and programs that passes for a system of global governance'.

NOTES

1 Canada and Mexico, bound to the US economy through the North American Free Trade Agreement, were much less affected 'due largely to tighter regulations and far less internationalized financial markets' (Farnsworth and Irving 2015, p. 63).

2 Jenson (2010) highlights the 'polysemic' nature of such names; in other words, such names are often sufficiently ambiguous as to appeal to diverse forces. See also Tag (2013).

3 Deacon here is using a concept drawn from Antonio Gramsci, which refers to a longer-term battle for ideological hegemony, carried out in the trench works of civil society.

4 Deacon does try to include gender and race-ethnicity in his framework but these are not treated as central to the 'war'.

5 See, inter alia, Weyland (2006, chapters 3 and 4), who documents the considerable friction these reform initiatives encountered even in countries that apparently followed the Bank's advice.

6 In addition to IOs and NGOs, the Kaasch and Martens (2015) volume includes the European Union, the BRICS and the G20 as agents or sites of agency.

7 Deacon is here referring to the World Bank's competition with the World Health Organization (health), United Nations Education, Science and Cultural Organization (education) and the ILO (social protection).

8 The MDGs' definition of reproductive health, with its emphasis on combating maternal mortality, however, pales in comparison to the third goal of the Sustainable Development Goals, agreed to in 2015. Goal 3.5 officially commits member countries to ensuring 'universal access to sexual and reproductive health care services, including family planning, information and education, and the integration of reproductive health into national strategies and programs' (UN Department of Economic and Social Affairs 2015).

9 On ECLAC's growing engagement in promoting social policy reform, see Mahon (2015).

10 For more information, see Transnational Institute (n.d.) and Peoples Agenda for Alternative Regionalisms (n.d.).

Conclusion

Over the last few decades, social policy has expanded dramatically as a research field. This is especially true of comparative welfare studies, which has broadened its reach to deal with all regions of the world. Without neglecting the contributions of the classics in this field, the eight chapters in this book have introduced current issues and perspectives that help us map the many challenges facing contemporary social policy practice and research.

First, compared to traditional introductions, this book has systematically acknowledged the contribution of feminist scholars to our understanding of welfare regimes and more broadly to social policy. Gender is a central category in contemporary social policy research, as the book shows in a variety of ways. Gender analysis has become and should remain part of mainstream social policy research.

Second, following the pioneering works of scholars like Fiona Williams (1995), our book has suggested that social policy research needs to take changing definitions of the nation and its boundaries more seriously. In an era of global immigration and economic pressures, the defining and redefining of national boundaries and membership are crucial processes that should move to the centre of contemporary welfare state analysis. These remarks apply to issues as varied as refugee settlement, economic migration, the global care chain and sub-state nationalism.

Third, the book invites students of social policy to pay close attention to the issue of global governance, especially the social policy role of international organizations and other transnational actors. To stress the growing import of what is known as global social policy (Deacon 2007) is not to deny that social policy remains the responsibility of national, and in some cases sub-national, states. Thus, global social policy ideas are unlikely to become a reality without the collaboration of national policy makers (Orenstein 2008). Differences among countries remain significant in key policy areas and comparative policy research aimed at explaining such differences remains essential. At the same time, social policy ideas travel in multiple directions. Therefore, it is increasingly important to take the transnational dimension into account.

Fourth, global social policy draws our attention to the fact that social policy is no longer a domain dominated entirely by advanced industrial, and especially European, countries. Countries from the Global South are now the site of significant social policy experiments, and the work being done by scholars in the South builds on and challenges the analytical and empirical knowledge generated in the Global North. This book has sought to make a strong case for continuing the dialogue between social policy scholars from the North and the South.

Finally, this book has made a strong case for the systematic study of the role of ideas in social policy. Ideas play a role in the cognitive, framing and discursive processes that take place in each country and also travel, albeit not 'friction-free', across the globe. The importance of ideas has been recognized in social policy research but it has yet to receive the attention devoted to institutional analysis or structural transformations. This is not to say that ideas are more important than actors and institutions in the shaping of welfare politics. Rather, we simply argue that a focus on ideas provides a useful complement to existing approaches to welfare state development, particularly as this relates to the issue of social policy change.

These five main contributions should not obscure the fact that the more traditional approaches, such as industrialism and power-resource theory, remain relevant to contemporary social policy research. Rather than pitting various perspectives against each other, we seek to create a fruitful dialogue among them. Such a dialogue requires analytical rigour, as well as a clear understanding of the boundaries demarcating existing approaches (Parsons 2007). When done with care, such an inclusive approach to social policy research can help to bridge gaps in available explanatory frameworks and build more sophisticated approaches to social policy development (Myles and Quadagno 2002).

Like all books, our text has clear limitations, which derive in part from the introductory nature of this project. Rather than reviewing all theories and concepts available in the literature, we decided to focus on those we find the most analytically and empirically fruitful. While this book has discussed a variety of empirical examples, it did not focus on any country or programmatic issue in depth in order to take a broader look at social policy issues as they emerge in a variety of national contexts.

In the years to come, it is likely that issues barely touched on or acknowledged in this book might become central to social policy debates. This is why students of social policy need always to remain on the lookout for emerging trends and issues. New empirical realities should lead scholars to revise their concepts or formulate new ones. For example, in the last decade, scholars such as Michael Cahill (2002), Tony Fitzpatrick (2011, 2014) and Ian Gough (2015) have started to explore the relationship between welfare, human need, and environmental issues such as climate change. Simultaneously, in the wake of the recent refugee crisis in Europe and the Middle East, more attention is being paid to migration as it intersects with both the politics of social policy and the rise of right-wing populism of the sort that triumphed in the United Kingdom in the June 2016 European Union membership referendum, resulting in the victory of the 'Brexit' camp. In addition, while the van Kersbergen and Manow (2009) volume *Religion, Class Coalitions, and Welfare States* explored the relationship between religion and social policy in the development of Western welfare states, the issue is becoming more pressing than ever, in a context of the enduring reliance of faith-based welfare in many countries (Jawad 2012) as well as the new prominence given to religious difference associated with migratory trends. Finally, issues of sexual identity and orientation are increasingly prevalent in contemporary social policy debates, as the quest for lesbian, gay, bisexual and transgender (LGBT) rights around the world intersects with core social policy issues such as equal access to cash benefits and health services, including for same-sex partners (Lind 2004).

These issues are related to the broader theme of social inclusion, which has become so central to global social policy debates over the last two decades (Béland 2007). At the same time, 'newer' problems should not displace classic social policy issues such as the fight against class and income inequality, which remains a key policy issue across the world. Economic inequality has been given new prominence by recent publications by Milanovic (2005), the OECD (2011, 2015) and Piketty (2014) as well as by social movements like those highlighted by the Occupy Movement that push to redistribute income from the 'top one percent'. Thus, more research is needed about the relationship between economic inequality, fiscal redistribution and social policy and progressive policy alternatives such as the idea of a basic or guaranteed minimum income for all citizens (Sheahen 2012).

As this book suggests, the field of social policy is hardly static and much progress has been made in recent decades, at both the empirical and the theoretical levels. Today we know more about social policy, both at home and around the world, than ever before. Such social policy knowledge is important because it can help us to better grasp key aspects of contemporary societies in historical and comparative perspective, while providing the tools to improve the social programs that matter so much in the daily lives of individuals and communities.

References

Abrahamson, Peter (1999), 'The welfare modelling business', *Social Policy and Administration*, **33** (4), 394–415.

Alesina, Alberto R. and Edward L. Glaeser (2004), *Fighting Poverty in the US and Europe: A World of Difference*, Oxford and New York: Oxford University Press.

Alesina, Alberto R. and Edward L. Glaeser (2008), 'Why are welfare states in the US and Europe so different? What do we learn?', *Horizons stratégiques: Revue trimestrielle du Centre d'analyse stratégique*, **2** (2), 51–61.

Armingeon, Klaus and Giuliano Bonoli (eds) (2006), *The Politics of Post-industrial Welfare States: Adapting Post-war Social Policies to New Social Risks*, London: Routledge.

Armstrong, Pat, A. Bannerjee, M. Szebehely, H. Armstrong, T. Daly and S. LaFrance (2009), *They Deserve Better: The Long Term Care Experience in Canada and Scandinavia*, Ottawa: Canadian Centre for Policy Alternatives.

Arts, Wil and John Gelissen (2002), 'Three worlds of welfare capitalism or more? A state-of-the-art report', *Journal of European Social Policy*, **12** (2), 137–58.

Ayhan, Berkay and Stephen McBride (2015), 'Global crisis and social policy in peripheral Europe: comparing Ireland, Portugal and Greece', in Stephen McBride, Rianne Mahon and Gerard Boychuk (eds), *After '08: Social Policy and the Global Financial Crisis*, Vancouver: UBC Press, pp. 237–53.

Baldwin, Peter (1990), *The Politics of Social Solidarity: Class Bases of the European Welfare State 1875–1975*, Cambridge and New York: Cambridge University Press.

Banting, Keith (2000), 'Looking in three directions: migration and the European welfare state in comparative perspective', in Michael Bommes and Andrew Geddes (eds), *Immigration and Welfare: Challenging the Borders of the Welfare State*, London: Routledge, pp. 13–33.

Banting, Keith (2005), 'Canada: nation-building in a federal welfare state', in Hans Obinger, Stefan Leibfried and Francis G. Castles (eds), *Federalism and the Welfare State: New World and European Experiences*, Cambridge and New York: Cambridge University Press, pp. 89–137.

Banting, Keith (2008), 'Canada as counter-narrative: multiculturalism, recognition and redistribution', in Richard Simeon, Robert Vipond and Linda White (eds), *The Comparative Turn in Canadian Political Science*, Vancouver: UBC Press, pp. 59–76.

Banting, Keith, Richard Johnston, Will Kylmicka and Stuart Soroka (2006), 'Do multiculturalism policies erode the welfare state? An empirical analysis', in Keith Banting and Will Kymlicka (eds), *Multiculturalism and the Welfare State: Recognition and Redistribution in Contemporary Democracies*, Oxford and New York: Oxford University Press, pp. 49–91.

Banting, Keith, S. Soroka and E. Koning (2013), 'Multicultural diversity and redistribution', in K. Banting and J. Myles (eds), *Inequality and the Fading of Redistributive Politics*, Vancouver: UBC Press, pp. 165–86.

Barrientos, Armando (2009), 'Labour markets and the (hyphenated) welfare regimes in Latin America', *Economy and Society*, **38** (17), 87–108.

Begg, Ian G. and Jos Berghman (2002), 'Introduction: EU social (exclusion) policy revisited?', *Journal of European Social Policy*, **12** (3), 179–94.

Béland, Daniel (2005a), 'Insecurity, citizenship, and globalization: the multiple faces of state protection', *Sociological Theory*, **23** (1), 25–41.

Béland, Daniel (2005b), 'Ideas and social policy: an institutionalist perspective', *Social Policy and Administration*, **39** (1), 1–18.

Béland, Daniel (2007), 'The social exclusion discourse: ideas and policy change', *Policy & Politics*, **35** (1), 123–39.

Béland, Daniel (2009), 'Gender, ideational analysis, and social policy', *Social Politics*, **16** (4), 558–81.

Béland, Daniel (2010a), *What is Social Policy? Understanding the Welfare State*, Cambridge: Polity.

Béland, Daniel (2010b), 'Reconsidering policy feedback: how policies affect politics', *Administration & Society*, **42** (5), 568–90.

Béland, Daniel and Robert Henry Cox (eds) (2011), *Ideas and Politics in Social Science Research*, Oxford and New York: Oxford University Press.

Béland, Daniel and Robert Henry Cox (2016), 'Ideas as coalition magnets: coalition building, policy entrepreneurs, and power relations', *Journal of European Public Policy*, **23** (3), 428–45.

Béland, Daniel and Brian Gran (eds) (2008), *Public and Private Social Policy: Health and Pension Policies in a New Era*, Basingstoke: Palgrave Macmillan.

Béland, Daniel and Randall Hansen (2000), 'Reforming the French welfare state: solidarity, social exclusion and the three crises of citizenship', *West European Politics*, **23** (1), 47–64.

Béland, Daniel and A. Lecours (2012), *Nationalism and Social Policy: The Politics of Territorial Solidarity*, Oxford and New York: Oxford University Press.

Béland, Daniel and Mitchell Orenstein (2013), 'International organizations as policy actors: an ideational approach', *Global Social Policy*, **13** (2), 125–43.

Béland, Daniel and Klaus Petersen (eds) (2014), *Analysing Social Policy Concepts and Language: Comparative and Transnational Perspectives*, Bristol: Policy Press.

Béland, Daniel and Alex Waddan (2012), *The Politics of Policy Change: Welfare, Medicare, and Social Security Reform in the United States*, Washington, DC: Georgetown University Press.

Béland, Daniel and Alex Waddan (2015), 'Breaking down ideas and institutions: the politics of tax policy in the U.S. and the U.K.', *Policy Studies*, **36** (2), 176–95.

Benería, Lourdes (2008), 'The crisis of care, international migration and public policy', *Feminist Economics*, **14** (3), 1–21.

Benford, Robert D. and David A. Snow (2000), 'Framing processes and social movements: an overview and assessment', *Annual Review of Sociology*, **26**, 611–39.

Bergqvist, Christina, Anette Borchost, Ann-Dorte Christensen, Viveca Ramstedt-Silén, Nina C. Raaum and Auour Styrkársdóttir (eds) (1999), *Equal Democracies? Gender and Politics in the Nordic Countries*, Oslo: Scandinavian University Press.

Bergqvist, Christina, Elin Bjarngaard and Per Zetterberg (2015), 'When class trumps sex: the social democratic intra-party struggle over extending parental leave quotas in Sweden', *Social Politics*, doi: 10.1093/sp/jxvo17.

Bettio, Francesca, Annamaria Simnazzi and Paulo Villa (2006), 'Change in care regimes and female migration: the "care drain" in the Mediterranean', *Journal of European Social Policy*, 16 (3), 271–85.

Beveridge, W. (1942), *Social Insurance and Allied Services*, London: HMSO.

Blofield, Merike and Juliana Martinez-Franzoni (2015), 'Maternalism, co-responsibility and social equity: a typology of work-family policies', *Social Politics*, 22 (1), 38–59.

Blyth, Mark (2001), 'The transformation of the Swedish Model: economic ideas, distributional conflict and institutional change', *World Politics*, 54 (October), 1–26.

Blyth, Mark (2002), *Great Transformations: Economic Ideas and Institutional Change in the Twentieth Century*, Cambridge and New York: Cambridge University Press.

Bonoli, Giuliano (2000), *The Politics of Pension Reform: Institutions and Policy Change in Western Europe*, Cambridge and New York: Cambridge University Press.

Bonoli, Giuliano (2005), 'The politics of the new social policies: providing coverage against new social risks in mature welfare states', *Policy & Politics*, 33 (3), 431–49.

Bonoli, Giuliano (2006), 'New social risks and the politics of post-industrial social policies', in Klaus Armingeon and Giuliano Bonoli (eds), *The Politics of Post-industrial Welfare States: Adapting Post-war Social Policies to New Social Risks*, London: Routledge, pp. 3–26.

Bonoli, Giuliano (2012), 'Active labour market policy and social investment: a changing relationship', in Nathalie Morel, Bruno Palier and Joakim Palme (eds), *Towards a Social Investment Welfare State? Ideas, Policies and Challenges*, Bristol: Policy Press, pp. 181–205.

Bonoli, Giuliano and David Natali (eds) (2012), *The Politics of the New Welfare State*, Oxford and New York: Oxford University Press.

Boris, Eileen and Jennifer Fish (2014), 'Slaves no more: making global standards for domestic workers', *Feminist Studies*, 40 (2), 411–43.

Bourgeois, Léon (1896), reprinted in 1998, *Solidarité*, Villeneuve d'Ascq: Presses Universitaires du Septentrion.

Boychuk, Gerard. (2015), 'US incremental social policy expansionism in response to the crisis', in Stephen McBride, Rianne Mahon and Gerard Boychuk (eds), *After '08: Social Policy and the Global Financial Crisis*, Vancouver: UBC Press, pp. 292–312.

Breitenbach, Dagmar (2016), 'Do migrants in Germany need sex education?', *Deutsche Welle*, 14 March, available at http://www.dw.com/en/do-migrants-in-germany-need-sex-education/a-19115638 (accessed 1 July 2016).

Brochmann, Grete (2015), 'Immigration and the Nordic welfare state: a tense companionship', in Pauli Kettunen, Sonya Michel and Klaus Petersen (eds), *Race, Ethnicity and Welfare States: An American Dilemma?*, Cheltenham, UK and Northampton, MA, USA: Edward Elgar Publishing, pp. 83–103.

Brodie, Janine and Jane Jenson (1988), *Crisis, Challenge and Change: Party and Class in Canada Revisited*, Ottawa: Carleton University Press.

Bulmer, Anthony and A. Martin Reeds (eds) (1996), *Citizenship Today: The Contemporary Relevance of T. H. Marshall*, London: UCL Press.

Burmeister Hicks, C. Jakob and André Somby (2005), 'Sami responses to poverty in the Nordic Countries', in Robyn Everside, John-Andres McNeish and Alberto D. Cimadamore (eds), *Indigenous Peoples and Poverty: An International Perspective*, London: Zed Books, pp. 274–89.

Cahill, Michael (2002), *The Environment and Social Policy*, London: Routledge.

Campbell, John L. (1998), 'Institutional analysis and the role of ideas in political economy', *Theory and Society*, **27**, 377–409.

Campbell, John L. (2004), *Institutional Change and Globalization*, Princeton, NJ: Princeton University Press.

Campbell, John L. and Ove K. Pedersen (2011), 'Knowledge regimes and comparative political economy', in Daniel Béland and Robert Henry Cox (eds), *Ideas and Politics in Social Science Research*, Oxford and New York: Oxford University Press, pp. 167–90.

Careja, Romana, Patrick Emmenegger and Jon Kvist (2015), 'An American dilemma in Europe? Welfare reform and immigration', in Pauli Kettunen, Sonya Michel and Klaus Petersen (eds), *Race, Ethnicity and Welfare States: An American Dilemma?*, Cheltenham, UK and Northampton, MA, USA: Edward Elgar Publishing, pp. 128–49.

Carstensen, Martin B. (2011), 'Paradigm man vs. the bricoleur: bricolage as an alternative vision of agency in ideational change', *European Political Science Review*, **3** (1), 147–67.

Castel, Robert (2003), *From Manual Workers to Wage Laborers: Transformation of the Social Question*, New Brunswick, NJ: Transaction Publishers.

Castles, Francis and Deborah Mitchell (1993), 'Worlds of welfare and families of nations', in Francis Castles (ed.), *Families of Nations: Patterns of Public Policy in Western Democracies*, Aldershot: Dartmouth, pp. 93–128.

Castles, Stephen, Carl-Ulrik Schierup and Peo Hansen (2006), *Migration, Citizenship and the European Welfare State: A European Dilemma*, London: Oxford University Press, available at http://www.oxfordscholarship.com (accessed 1 July 2016).

Cerny, Philip (1997), 'Paradoxes of the competition state: dynamics of political globalization', *Government and Opposition*, **35** (2), 251–74.

Clarke, John and Janet Newman (1997), *The Managerial State: Power, Politics and Ideology in the Remaking of Social Welfare*, London: Sage.

Clarke, John, Dave Bainton, Noémi Lendvai and Paul Stubbs (2015), *Making Policy Move: Towards a Politics of Travel and Assemblage*, Bristol: Policy Press.

Clarke, Marlea (2015), 'Social policy in South Africa: cushioning the blow of the recession?', in Stephen McBride, Rianne Mahon and Gerard Boychuk (eds), *After '08: Social Policy and the Global Financial Crisis*, Vancouver: UBC Press, pp. 197–215.

Conway, Janet (2012), *Edges of Global Justice: The World Social Forum and Its 'Others'*, New York: Routledge.

Cook, Sarah and Wing Lam (2015), 'In the shadow of crisis: change and continuity in China's post crisis social policy', in Stephen McBride, Rianne Mahon and Gerard Boychuk (eds), *After '08: Social Policy and the Global Financial Crisis*, Vancouver: UBC Press, pp. 216–34.

Cox, Robert Henry (2001), 'The social construction of an imperative: why welfare reform happened in Denmark and the Netherlands but not in Germany', *World Politics*, **53**, 463–98.

Cox, Robert Henry (2004), 'The path dependence of an idea: why Scandinavian welfare states remain distinct', *Social Policy and Administration*, **38** (2), 204–19.

Craig, Doug and David Porter (2004), 'The Third Way and the Third World: poverty reduction and social inclusion in the rise of "inclusive liberalism"', *Review of International Political Economy*, **11** (2), 387–423.

Crouch, Colin and Maarten Keune (2005), 'Changing dominant practice: making use of institutional diversity in Hungary and the United Kingdom', in W. Streeck and K. Thelen (eds), *Beyond Continuity: Institutional Change in Advanced Political Economies*, Oxford and New York: Oxford University Press, pp. 83–102.

Da Roit, Barbara and Stefania Sabatelli (2013), 'Nothing on the move or just going private? Understanding the freeze on child and eldercare policies and the development of care markets in Italy', *Social Politics*, **20** (3), 430–53.

DAC (1996), *Shaping the 21st Century: The Contribution of Development Assistance*, Paris: OECD.

Daly, Mary (2011), 'What adult earner model? A critical look at recent social policy reform in Europe from a gender and family perspective', *Social Politics*, **18** (1), 1–23.

Daly, Mary and Jane Lewis (2000), 'The concept of social care and the analysis of contemporary welfare states', *British Journal of Sociology*, **51** (2), 281–98.

Deacon, Bob (2000), 'Eastern European welfare states: the impact of the politics of globalization', *Journal of European Social Policy*, **10** (2), 146–61.

Deacon, Bob (2007), reprinted in 2008, *Global Social Policy and Governance*, London: Sage.

Deacon, Bob (2013), *Global Social Policy in the Making: The Foundations of the Social Protection Floor*, Bristol: Policy Press.

Deacon, Bob (2014), 'Career, charisma, conviction and the challenges facing the SPF', *Global Social Policy*, **14** (3), 406–16.

Deacon, Bob and Maria Cristina Macovei (2010), 'Regional social policy from above: international organizations and regional social policy', in B. Deacon (ed.), *World-regional Social Policy and Global Governance: New Research and Policy Agendas in Africa, Asia, Europe and Latin America*, London: Routledge, pp. 63–85.

Deacon, Bob, with Michelle Hulse and Paul Stubbs (1997), *Global Social Policy: International Organisations and the Future of Welfare*, London: Sage.

Dean, Hartley (1996) *Welfare Law and Citizenship*, Hamel Hempstead: Harvester Wheatsheaf.

Dimaria, Federico, Francois Schneider, Filka Sekalova and Joan Martinez-Alier (2013), 'What is de-growth? From an activist slogan to a social movement', *Environmental Values*, **22** (2), 191–215.

Domhoff, William (1970), *The Higher Circles: The Ruling Class in America*, New York: Random House.

Domhoff, William (1996), *State Autonomy or Class Dominance? Case Studies on Policy Making in America*, New York: Aldine de Gruyter.

Dufour, Pascale, Dominique Masson and Dominique Caouette (2010), *Solidarity Beyond Borders: Transnational Women's Movements*, Vancouver: UBC Press.

Durkheim, Émile (1893), reprinted in 1997, *The Division of Labor in Society*, New York: Free Press.

Dwyer, Peter (2004), 'Creeping conditionality in the UK: from welfare rights to conditional entitlements?', *Canadian Journal of Sociology*, **28** (2), 261–83.

ECORYS (2011), *Evaluation of the European Year 2010 for Combating Poverty and Social Exclusion*, Brussels: European Commission.

Edsall, T.B. (2014), 'The rise of "welfare chauvinism"', *New York Times*, 16 December, available at http://www.nytimes.com/2014/12/17/opinion/the-rise-of-welfare-chauvinism.html?_r=0 (accessed 1 July 2016).

Ellingsaeter, Anne Lise (2014), 'Nordic earner–carer models—why stability and instability?', *Journal of Social Policy*, **43** (3), 555–74.

Esping-Andersen, Gøsta (1985a), *Politics Against Markets: The Social Democratic Road to Power*, Princeton, NJ: Princeton University Press.

Esping-Andersen, Gøsta (1985b), 'Power and distributional regimes', *Politics and Society*, **14** (2), 223–56.

Esping-Andersen, Gøsta (1990), *The Three Worlds of Welfare Capitalism*, Princeton, NJ: Princeton University Press.

Esping-Andersen, Gøsta (1997), 'Hybrid or unique? The Japanese welfare state between Europe and America', *Journal of European Social Policy*, **7** (3), 179–89.

Esping-Andersen, Gøsta (1999), *Social Foundations of Postindustrial Economies*, Oxford and New York: Oxford University Press.

Esping-Andersen, Gøsta (2002), 'A child centred social investment strategy', in Gøsta Esping-Andersen, Duncan Gallie, Anton Hemerijk and John Myers (eds), *Why We Need a New Welfare State*, Oxford and New York: Oxford University Press, pp. 26–67.

Esping-Andersen, Gøsta (2009), *Incomplete Revolution: Adapting Welfare States to Women's New Roles*, Cambridge: Polity.

Estévez-Abe, Margarita and Yeong Soon Kim (2014), 'Presidents, prime ministers and the politics of care—why Korea expanded child care much more than Japan', *Social Policy and Administration*, **48** (6), 666–85.

European Parliament (2014), 'The open method of coordination', available at http://www.europarl.europa.eu/EPRS/EPRS-AaG-542142-Open-Method-of-Coordination-FINAL.pdf (accessed 10 January 2016).

Evans, Peter B., Dietrich Rueschemeyer and Theda Skocpol (eds) (1985), *Bringing the State Back In*, Cambridge and New York: Cambridge University Press.

Ewald, François (1986), *L'État providence*, Paris: Grasset.

Eydal, Gyoný Björk and Tine Rostgaard (2011), 'Gender equality revisted—changes in Nordic childcare policies in the 2000s', *Social Politics and Administration*, **45** (2), 161–79.

Fargion, Valeria (2000), 'Timing and the development of social care services in Europe', *West European Politics*, **23** (2), 59–88.

Farnsworth, Kevin and Zoë Irving (2015), 'A new era for social policy? Welfare states and the financial crisis', in Stephen McBride, Rianne Mahon and Gerard Boychuk (eds), *After '08: Social Policy and the Global Financial Crisis*, Vancouver: UBC Press, pp. 59–84.

Faur, Eleonor (2011), 'A widening gap? The political and social organization of child care in Argentina', *Development and Change*, **42** (4), 967–94.

Fenwick, Tracy Beck (2010), 'The institutional feasibility of national-local policy collaboration: insights from Brazil and Argentina', *Journal of Politics in Latin America*, **2** (2), 155–83.

Fenwick, Tracy Beck (2016), *Avoiding Governors: Federalism, Democracy, and Poverty Alleviation in Brazil and Argentina*, South Bend, IN: University of Notre Dame Press.

Fernández de la Hoz, Paloma (2001), *Families and Social Exclusion in the European Union: Theoretical Aspects, Lines of Convergence and Unsettled Issues—Abridged Version*, Vienna: European Observatory on the Social Situation, Demography and Family.

Ferragina, Emanuele and Martin Seeleib-Kaiser (2015), 'Determinants of a silent revolution: understanding the expansion of family policies in rich OECD countries', *Social Politics*, **22** (1), 1–37.

Ferrera, Maurizio (1996), 'The "Southern Model" of welfare regimes in social Europe', *Journal of European Social Policy*, **6** (1), 17–36.

Ferrera, Maurizio and Anton Hemerijck (2003), 'Recalibrating Europe's welfare regimes', in Jonathan Zeitlin and David Trubeck (eds), *Governing Work and Welfare in a New Economy*, Oxford and New York: Oxford University Press, pp. 88–128.

Filgueira, Fernando (2005), *Welfare and Democracy in Latin America: The Development, Crises and Aftermath of Universal, Dual and Exclusionary Welfare States*, Geneva: UNRISD.

Finkel, Alvin (2006), *Social Policy and Practice in Canada: A History*, Waterloo: Wilfrid Laurier University Press.

Fitzpatrick, Tony (2011), *Understanding the Environment and Social Policy*, Bristol: Policy Press.

Fitzpatrick, Tony (2014), *Climate Change and Poverty: A New Agenda for Developed Nations*, Bristol: Policy Press.

Fleckenstein, Timo and Martin Seeleib-Kaiser (2011), 'Business, skills and the welfare state: the political economy of employment oriented family policy in Britain and Germany', *Journal of European Social Policy*, **21** (2), 136–49.

Fleckenstein, Timo and Soohyun Christine Lee (2014), 'The politics of postindustrial social policy: family policy reforms in Britain, Germany, South Korea and Sweden', *Comparative Political Studies*, **47** (4), 601–30.

Foucault, Michael (1980), *Power/Knowledge: Selected Interviews and Other Writings, 1972–1977*, ed. Colin Gordon, New York: Pantheon Books.

Fraser, Nancy (1997), *Justice Interruptus: Critical Reflections on the 'Postsocialist' Condition*, New York: Routledge.

Fraser, Nancy and Linda Gordon (1994), '"Dependency" demystified: inscriptions of power in a keyword of the welfare state', *Social Politics*, **1** (1), 4–31.

Frétigné, Cédric (1999), *Sociologie de l'exclusion*, Paris: L'Harmattan.

Friesen, Elizabeth (2012), *Challenging Global Finance: Civil Society and Transnational Networks*, Basingstoke: Palgrave Macmillan.

Fukuda-Parr, Sakiko and David Hulme (2011), 'International norm dynamics and the "end of poverty": understanding the Millennium Development Goals', *Global Governance*, **17**, 17–36.

Gal, John (1996), 'Is there an extended family of Mediterranean welfare states?', *Journal of European Social Policy*, **20** (4), 283–300.

Gallie, Duncan, Serge Paugam and Sheila Jacobs (2003), 'Unemployment, poverty and social isolation: is there a vicious circle of social exclusion?', *European Societies*, **5** (1), 1–31.

Garrett, Geoff (1998), 'Global markets and national policies: collision course or virtuous circle?', *International Organization*, **52** (4) 787–824.

Goguel d'Allondans, Alban (2003), *L'exclusion sociale: les métamorphoses d'un concept (1960–2000)*, Paris: L'Harmattan.

Goodliffe, Gabriel (2012), *The Resurgence of the Radical Right in France: From Boulangisme to the Front National*, Cambridge and New York: Cambridge University Press.

Goodman, Roger and Ito Peng (1996), 'Peripatetic learning, adaptive change and nation-building', in Gøsta Esping-Andersen (ed.), *Welfare States in Transition: National Adaptations in Global Economies*, London: UNRISD/Sage, pp. 192–224.

Gordon, Colin (1991), 'New Deal, old deck: business and the origins of Social Security, 1920–1935', *Politics and Society*, **19**, 165–207.

Gorfinkel, Magdalena Díaz and Ángela Escrivá (2012), 'Care of older people in migration contexts: local and transnational arrangements', *Social Politics*, **19** (1), 129–41.

Gough, Ian (1979), *The Political Economy of the Welfare State*, London: Macmillan.

Gough, Ian (2015), 'Climate change and sustainable welfare: the centrality of human needs', *Cambridge Journal of Economics*, doi: 10.1093/cje/bev039.

Guillén, Ana and Emmanuele Pavolini (2015), 'Welfare states under strain in Southern Europe: overview of the Special Issue', *European Journal of Social Security*, **17** (2), 147–57.

Hacker, Björn (2009), 'Hybridization instead of clustering: transformation processes of welfare policies in Central and Eastern Europe', *Social Policy and Administration*, **43** (2), 152–69.

Hacker, Jacob S. (2002), *The Divided Welfare State: The Battle Over Public and Private Social Benefits in the United States*, Cambridge and New York: Cambridge University Press.

Hacker, Jacob S. (2004), 'Privatizing risk without privatizing the welfare state: the hidden politics of welfare state retrenchment in the United States', *American Political Science Review*, **98**, 243–60.

Hacker, Jacob S. (2006), *The Great Risk Shift*, Oxford and New York: Oxford University Press.

Hacker, Jacob S. and Paul Pierson (2002), 'Business power and social policy: employers and the formation of the American welfare state', *Politics and Society*, **30** (2), 277–325.

Haggard, Stephan and Robert Kaufman (2008), *Development, Democracy and Welfare States: Latin America, East Asia and Eastern Europe*, Princeton, NJ: Princeton University Press.

Hall, Peter A. (1993), 'Policy paradigms, social learning and the state: the case of economic policymaking in Britain', *Comparative Politics*, **25** (3), 275–96.

Hall, Peter A. and David Soskice (eds) (2001), 'An introduction to Varieties of Capitalism', in Peter A. Hall and David Soskice (eds), *Varieties of Capitalism: The Institutional Foundations of Comparative Advantage*, Oxford and New York: Oxford University Press, pp. 1–68.

Hanlon, Joseph, Armando Barrientos and David Hulme (2013), *Just Give Money to the Poor: The Development Revolution from the Global South*, Boulder, CO and London: Kumarian Press/Lynne Rienner.

Hay, Colin (2011), 'Ideas and the construction of interests', in Daniel Béland and Robert H. Cox (eds), *Ideas and Politics in Social Science Research*, Oxford and New York: Oxford University Press, pp. 65–82.

Hayek, Friedrich A. (1944), reprinted in 2007, *The Road to Serfdom: Text and Documents—The Definitive Edition*, Chicago, IL: University of Chicago Press.

Hayward, Jack (1959), 'Solidarity: the social history of an idea in nineteenth century France', *International Review of Social History*, **4**, 261–84.

Hennock, E.P. (2007), *The Origin of the Welfare State in England and Germany, 1850–1914. Social Policies Compared*, Cambridge and New York: Cambridge University Press.

Hills, John (2004), *Inequality and the State*, Oxford: Oxford University Press.

Hills, John, Julian Le Grand and David Piachaud (eds) (2002), *Understanding Social Exclusion*, Oxford and New York: Oxford University Press.

Hochschild, Arlie R (2000), 'Global care chains and emotional surplus value', in William Hutton and Anthony Giddens (eds), *On the Edge: Living with Global Capitalism*, London: Jonathan Cape, pp. 130–46.

Holliday, Ian (2000), 'Productivist welfare capitalism: social policy in East Asia', *Political Studies*, **48**, 706–23.

Hong, Liu and Kristian Kongshøj (2014), 'China's welfare reforms: an ambiguous road towards a social protection floor', *Global Social Policy*, **14** (3), 352–68.

Howard, Christopher (1997), *The Hidden Welfare State: Tax Expenditures and Social Policy in the United States*, Princeton, NJ: Princeton University Press.

Howard, Christopher (2006), *The Welfare State Nobody Knows: Debunking Myths about U.S. Social Policy*, Princeton, NJ: Princeton University Press.

Huber, Evelyne and John D. Stephens (2001), *Development and Crisis of the Welfare State: Parties and Policies in Global Markets*, Chicago, IL: University of Chicago Press.

Huber, Evelyne and John Stephens (2012), *Democracy and the Left: Social Policy and Inequality in Latin America*, Chicago, IL and London: University of Chicago Press.

Hudson, John (2012), 'Welfare regimes and global cities: a missing link in the comparative analysis of welfare states', *Journal of Social Policy*, **41** (3), 455–73.

Humpage, Louise (2010), 'Institutions, interests *and* ideas: explaining social policy change in welfare states incorporating an indigenous population', *Journal of European Social Policy*, **20** (3), 235–47.

ILO (2011), *Social Protection Floor for a Fair and Inclusive Globalization: Report of the Social Protection Floor Advisory Group*, Geneva: International Labour Organization.

Immergut, Ellen M. (1998), 'The theoretical core of institutionalism', *Politics and Society*, **26**, 5–34.

Jacobs, Alan M. (2009), 'How do ideas matter? Mental models and attention in German pension politics', *Comparative Political Studies*, **42** (2), 252–79.

Javornik, Jana (2014), 'Measuring state familialism: contesting postsocialist exceptionalism', *Journal of European Social Policy*, **24** (3), 240–57.

Jawad, Rana (2012), *Religion and Faith Based Welfare: From Wellbeing to Ways of Being*, Bristol: Policy Press.

Jenson, Jane (1989), 'Paradigms and political discourse: protective legislation in France and the United States before 1914', *Canadian Journal of Political Science*, **22** (2), 235–58.

Jenson, Jane (1997), 'Who cares? Gender and welfare regimes', *Social Politics*, **4** (2), 182–7.

Jenson, Jane (2004), *Canada's New Social Risks: Directions for a New Social Architecture*, Ottawa: Canadian Policy Research Networks.

Jenson, Jane (2009), 'Lost in translation: the social investment perspective and gender equality', *Social Politics*, **16** (4), 446–83.

Jenson, Jane (2010), 'Diffusing ideas for after neoliberalism: the social investment perspective in Europe and Latin America', *Global Social Policy*, **10** (1), 59–84.

Jenson, Jane and Denis Saint Martin (2003), 'New routes of social cohesion? Citizenship and the social investment state', *Canadian Journal of Sociology*, **28** (1), 77–99.

Jones, Catherine (1993), 'The Pacific challenge', in Catherine Jones (ed.), *New Perspectives on the Welfare State in Europe*, London: Routledge, pp. 198–217.

Kaasch, Alexandra and Kerstin Martens (eds) (2015), *Actors and Agency in Global Social Governance*, Oxford: Oxford University Press.

Kalecki, Michael (1942), 'Political aspects of full employment', reprinted in 1972, in E.K. Hunt (ed.), *A Critique of Economic Theory*, London: Penguin.

Katz, Michael B. (2008), *The Price of Citizenship: Redefining the American Welfare State*, Philadelphia: University of Pennsylvania Press.

Keck, Margaret and Kathryn Sikkink (1999), 'Transnational advocacy networks in international and regional politics', *International Social Science Journal*, **51** (159), 89–101.

Keil, Roger and Rianne Mahon (2009), *Leviathan Undone? Towards a Political Economy of Scale*, Vancouver: UBC Press.

Kerr, Clark, John Dunlop, Frederick Harbison and Charles Myers (1960), *Industrialism and Industrial Man*, Oxford and New York: Oxford University Press.

Kiliç, Sevgi, Sawitri Saharso and Birgit Sauer (2008), 'Introduction: the veil: debating citizenship, gender and religious diversity', *Social Politics*, **15** (4), 397–410.

Kingdon, John W. (1984), *Agendas, Alternatives, and Public Policies*, Boston, MA: Little, Brown Book Group.

Kingfisher, Catherine (2013), *A Policy Travelogue: Tracing Welfare Reform in Aotearoa/New Zealand and Canada*, New York and Oxford: Berghahn.

Klanfer, Jules (1965), *L'Exclusion sociale: Étude de la marginalité dans les sociétés occidentales*, Paris: Bureau de Recherches sociales.

Knijn, Trudie and Leila Patel (2012), 'Introduction: social policy change in a transitional-society—the case of South Africa', *Social Policy and Administration*, **46** (6), 597–602.

Korpi, Walter (1978), *The Working Class in Welfare Capitalism: Work, Unions and Politics in Sweden*, London: Routledge and Kegan Paul.

Korpi, Walter (1980), 'Social policy and distributional conflict in the capitalist democracies. A preliminary comparative framework', *West European Politics*, 3 (3), 296–315.

Korpi, Walter (1983), *The Democratic Class Struggle*, London: Routledge and Kegan Paul.

Korpi, Walter (2000), 'Faces of inequality: gender, class and patterns of inequality in different types of welfare state', *Social Politics*, 7 (2), 127–91.

Korpi, Walter (2006), 'Power resources and employer centred approaches in explaining welfare states and varieties of capitalism: protagonists, consenters and antagonists', Paper presented at the ESPANet conference, University of Bremen, 21–23 September.

Kpessa, M.W., D. Béland and A. Lecours (2011), 'Nationalism, development, and social policy: the politics of nation-building in Sub-Saharan Africa', *Ethnic and Racial Studies*, 34 (12), 2115–33.

Kremer, Monique (2006), 'The politics of ideals of care: Danish and Flemish child care policy compared', *Social Politics*, 13 (2), 261–85.

Kuhn, Thomas S. (1962), *The Structure of Scientific Revolutions*, Chicago, IL: University of Chicago Press.

Lasswell, Harold D. (1936), *Politics: Who Gets What, When and How*, New York: Whittlesey House, McGraw-Hill.

Le Bihan, Blanche and Claude Martin (2006), 'A comparative case study of care systems for frail elderly people: Germany, Spain, France, Italy, the United Kingdom and Sweden', *Social Policy and Administration*, 40 (1), 26–46.

Lecours, A. and G. Nootens (2011), 'Understanding majority nationalism', in A.-G. Gagnon, G. Nootens and A. Lecours (eds), *Contemporary Majority Nationalism*, Montreal and Kingston: McGill-Queens University Press, pp. 3–18.

Leibfried, Stephan (1992), 'Towards a European welfare state?', in Zsuzsa Ferge and Jon Eivind Kolberg (eds), *Social Policy in a Changing Europe*, Frankfurt am Main: Campus Verlag, pp. 245–79.

Leitner, Sigrid (2003), 'Varieties of familialism: the caring function of the family in comparative perspective', *European Societies*, 5 (4), 353–75.

Leitner, Sigrid (2010), 'Germany outpaces Austria and childcare policy: the historical contingency of "conservative" childcare policies', *Journal of European Social Policy*, 20 (5), 456–67.

Leney, Tom (1999), 'European approaches to social exclusion', in Annette Hayton (ed.), *Tackling Disaffection and Social Exclusion: Education Perspectives and Policies*, London: Routledge, pp. 3–45.

Lenoir, René (1974), *Les exclus: un Français sur dix*, Paris: Le Seuil.

León, Margareta, Emmanuele Pavolini and Ana Guillén (2015), 'Welfare rescaling in Italy and Spain: political strategies to deal with harsh austerity', *European Journal of Social Security*, 17 (2), 182–201.

Leschke, Janine and Maria Jepsen (2014), 'Is economic crisis the prevailing gender regime? A comparison of Denmark, Germany, Slovenia and the United Kingdom', *Social Politics*, 20 (4), 485–508.

Levine, Daniel (1988), *Poverty and Society: The Growth of the American Welfare State in International Comparison*, New Brunswick, NJ: Rutgers University Press.

Levitas, Ruth (1999), reprinted in 2005, *Inclusive Society? Social Exclusion and New Labour* (second edn), Basingstoke: Palgrave Macmillan.

Levy, Denise Urias and Sonya Michel (2002), 'More can be less: child care and welfare reform in the United States', in S. Michel and R. Mahon (eds), *Child Care Policy at the Crossroads: Gender and Welfare State Restructuring*, New York and London: Routledge, pp. 239–63.

Lewis, Jane (1992), 'Gender and the development of welfare regimes', *Journal of European Social Policy*, **2** (1), 159–73.

Lewis, Jane (2008), 'Work-family balance policies: issues and development in the United Kingdom, 1997–2005 in comparative perspective', in J. Scott, S. Dex and H. Joshi (eds), *Women and Employment: Changing Lives and New Challenges*, Cheltenham, UK and Northampton, MA, USA: Edward Elgar Publishing, pp. 268–86.

Lewis, Jane and Ilona Ostner (1995), 'Gender and the evolution of European social policy', in S. Leibfried and P. Pierson (eds), *European Social Policy: Between Fragmentation and Integration*, Washington, DC: Brookings Institute, pp. 159–93.

Lieberman, R.C. (1998), *Shifting the Color Line: Race and the American Welfare State*, Cambridge, MA: Harvard University Press.

Lind, Amy (2004), 'Legislating the family: heterosexist bias in social welfare policy frameworks', *Journal of Sociology & Social Welfare*, **31** (4), 21–35.

Lipset, Seymour Martin (1990), *Continental Divide: The Values and Institutions of the United States and Canada*, New York: Routledge.

Lister, Ruth (1994), '"She has other duties"—women, citizenship and social security', in S. Baldwin and J. Falkingham (eds), *Social Security and Social Change: New Challenges to the Beveridge Model*, Hempel Hempstead: Harvester Wheatsheaf, pp. 31–44.

Lister, Ruth (1997), *Citizenship: Feminist Perspectives*, Basingstoke: Palgrave Macmillan.

Lister, Ruth (2009), 'A Nordic nirvana? Gender, citizenship and social justice in the Nordic welfare states', *Social Politics*, **19** (2), 242–78.

Lister, Ruth (2010), *Understanding Theories and Concepts in Social Policy*, Bristol: Policy Press.

Lister, Ruth, Fiona Williams, Anneli Anttonen et al. (2007), *Gendering Citizenship in Western Europe: New Challenges for Citizenship Research in a Cross-national Context*, Bristol: Policy Press.

Lopreite, Debora and Laura Macdonald (2014), 'Gender and Latin American welfare regimes: early childhood education and care in Argentina and Mexico', *Social Politics*, **21** (1), 80–102.

Luccisano, Lucy and Laura Macdonald (2012), 'The limits of anti-poverty policy: citizenship, accountability and neo-conservatism in Mexico's *Oportunidades* program', in Jordi Diaz and Susan Franceschet (eds), *Comparative Public Policy in Latin America*, Toronto: University of Toronto Press, pp. 205–27.

Lutz, Helma and Ewa Palenga-Möllenbeck (2012), 'Care workers, care drain and care chains: reflections on care, migration and citizenship', *Social Politics*, **19** (1), 15–37.

Mahon, Rianne (1997), 'Child care in Canada and Sweden: politics and policy', *Social Politics*, **4** (3), 382–418.

Mahon, Rianne (2002), 'Child care: toward what kind of "social Europe"?', *Social Politics*, **9** (3), 343–79.

Mahon, Rianne (2013), 'Social investment according to the OECD/DELSA: a discourse in the making', *Global Policy*, **4** (2), 150–59.

Mahon, Rianne (2014), 'The OECD's search for a new social policy language: from welfare state to active society', in Daniel Béland and Klaus Petersen (eds), *Analysing Social Policy Concepts and Language: Comparative and Transnational Perspectives*, Bristol: Policy Press, pp. 81–100.

Mahon, Rianne (2015), 'Integrating the social into CEPAL's neo-structuralist discourse', *Global Social Policy*, **15** (1), 3–22.

Mahon, Rianne (2016), 'Early childhood education and care in global discourses', in Karen Mundy, Alan Green, Robert Lingard and Antoni Verger (eds), *The Handbook of Global Politics and Policy-making in Education*, London: Wiley-Blackwell, pp. 224–40.

Mahon, Rianne and Deborah Brennan (2013), 'State structures and the politics of child-care: Australia and Canada', *Publius*, **43** (1), 90–108.

Mahon, Rianne, Anneli Anttonen, Deborah Brennan, Christina Bergqvist and Barbara Hobson (2012), 'Convergent care regimes? Child care in Australia, Canada, Finland and Sweden', *Journal of European Social Policy*, **22** (4), 419–31.

Mahon, Rianne, Christina Bergqvist and Deborah Brennan (2016), 'Social policy change: work-family tensions in Sweden, Australia and Canada', *Social Policy and Administration*, **50** (2), 224–40.

Mahoney, James and Kathleen Thelen (eds) (2009), *Explaining Institutional Change: Ambiguity, Agency, and Power*, Cambridge and New York: Cambridge University Press.

Maioni, Antonia (1998), *Parting at the Crossroads: The Emergence of Health Insurance in the United States and Canada*, Princeton, NJ: Princeton University Press.

Mares, Isabela (2003), *The Politics of Social Risk: Business and Welfare State Development*, Cambridge and New York: Cambridge University Press.

Marshall, T.H. (1964), 'Citizenship and social class', in T.H. Marshall, *Class, Citizenship and Development*, Garden City, NY: Doubleday, pp. 65–122.

Martin, Andrew (1975), 'Is democratic control of capitalist economies possible?', in Leon Lindberg and Claus Offe (eds), *Stress and Contradiction in Modern Capitalism: Public Policy and the Theory of the State*, Lexington, MA: Heath, pp. 13–56.

Martin, Andrew (1979), 'The dynamics of change in a Keynesian political economy: the Swedish case and its implications', in Colin Crouch (ed.), *State and Economy in Contemporary Capitalism*, London: Croom Helm, pp. 88–121.

Martin, Isaac William, Ajay K. Mehrotra and Monica Prasad (eds) (2009), *The New Fiscal Sociology: Taxation in a Comparative and Historical Perspective*, Cambridge and New York: Cambridge University Press.

Martinez-Franzoni, Juliana (2008), 'Welfare regimes in Latin America: capturing constellations of markets, families and policies', *Latin American Politics and Society*, **50** (2), 67–100.

Marx, Karl and Friedrich Engels (1848), reprinted in 1888, *Manifesto of the Communist Party*, Project Gutenberg EBook released in 2005, available at http://www.gutenberg.org/ebooks/61 (accessed 1 July 2016).

Marx Ferree, Myra and Aili Mari Tripp (2006), *Global Feminism: Transnational Women's Activism, Organizing and Human Rights*, New York: New York University Press.

Mätzke, Margitta and Ilona Ostner (2010), 'Postscript: ideas and agents of change in time', *Journal of European Social Policy*, **20** (5), 468–76.

McAdam, Douglas (1999), 'Conceptual issues, current problems, future direction', in Douglas McAdam, John D. McCarthy and Mayer N. Zald (eds), *Comparative Perspectives on Social Movements: Political Opportunities, Mobilizing Structure and Cultural Framings*, Cambridge and New York: Cambridge University Press, pp. 23–40.

McBride, Stephen (2015), 'Neo-liberalism in question?', in Stephen McBride, Rianne Mahon and Gerard Boychuk (eds), *After '08: Social Policy and the Global Financial Crisis*, Vancouver: UBC Press, pp. 21–39.

McEwen, N. (2006), *Nationalism and the State: Welfare and Identity in Scotland and Quebec*, Brussels: Peter Lang.

McLaughlin, Eithne and Caroline Glendinning (1994), 'Paying for care in Europe: is there a feminist approach?', in Linda Hantrais and Steen Mangen (eds), *Family Policy and the Welfare of Women*, Loughborough: Cross-National Research Group, pp. 52–69.

Mehta, Jal (2011), 'The varied roles of ideas in politics: from "whether" to "how"', in Daniel Béland and Robert H. Cox (eds), *Ideas and Politics in Social Science Research*, Oxford and New York: Oxford University Press, pp. 23–46.

Michel, Sonya and Ito Peng (2012), 'All in the family: migration, nationhood and care regimes in Asia and North America', *Journal of European Social Policy*, **22** (4), 406–18.

Milanovic, Branko (2005), *Worlds Apart: Measuring International and Global Inequality*, Princeton, NJ: Princeton University Press.

Mink, Gwendolyn (1998), *Welfare's End*, Ithaca, NY: Cornell University Press.

Mishra, Ramesh (1999), *Globalization and the Welfare State*, Cheltenham, UK and Northampton, MA, USA: Edward Elgar Publishing.

Molyneux, Maxine (2006), 'Mothers at the service of the new poverty agenda: Progresa/Oportunidades, Mexico's conditional transfer program', *Social Policy and Administration*, **40** (4), 425–41.

Morel, Nathalie (2015), 'Servants for the knowledge-based economy? The political economy of domestic services in Europe', *Social Politics*, **22** (2), 170–92.

Morel, Nathalie, Bruno Palier and Joakim Palme (2012a), 'Social investment: a paradigm in search of a new economic model and political mobilisation', in Nathalie Morel, Bruno Palier and Joakim Palme (eds), *Towards a Social Investment Welfare State? Ideas, Policies and Challenges*, Bristol: Bristol University Press, pp. 353–76.

Morel, Nathalie, Bruno Palier and Joakim Palme (2012b), 'Beyond the welfare state as we knew it?', in Nathalie Morel, Bruno Palier and Joakim Palme (eds), *Towards a Social Investment Welfare State? Ideas, Policies and Challenges*, Bristol: Policy Press, pp. 1–30.

Morgan, Kimberly (2006), *Working Mothers and the Welfare State: Religion and the Politics of Work-family Policies in Western Europe and the United States*, Stanford, CA: Stanford University Press.

Morgan, Kimberly (2009), 'Caring time policies in Western Europe: trends and implications', *Comparative European Politics*, **7**, 37–55.

Mossberger, Karen and Harold Wolman (2003), 'Policy transfer as a form of prospective policy evaluation: challenges and recommendations', *Public Administration Review*, **63** (4), 428–40.

Muller, Pierre (2005), 'Esquisse d'une théorie du changement dans l'action publique: structures, acteurs et cadres cognitifs', *Revue française de science politique*, **55** (1), 155–87.

Myles, John (1998), 'How to design a "liberal" welfare state: a comparison of Canada and the United States', *Social Policy and Administration*, **32** (4), 341–64.

Myles, John and Jill Quadagno (2002), 'Political theories of the welfare state', *Social Service Review*, **76** (1), 34–57.

Myles, John and Sébastien St Arnaud (2006), 'Population diversity, multiculturalism, and the welfare state: should welfare state theory be revised?', in Keith Banting and Will Kymlicka (eds), *Multiculturalism and the Welfare State: Recognition and Redistribution in Contemporary Democracies*, Oxford and New York: Oxford University Press, pp. 339–54.

Noël, Alain (2006), 'A new global politics of poverty', *Global Social Policy*, **6**, 304–33.

O'Connor, James (1973) *The Fiscal Crisis of the State*, New York: St Martin's Press.

O'Connor, Julia S. (1993), 'Gender, class and citizenship in the comparative analysis of welfare state regimes: theoretical and methodological issues', *British Journal of Sociology*, **44** (3), 501–18.

O'Connor, Julia S., Ann Shola Orloff and Sheila Shaver (1999), *States, Markets, Families: Gender, Liberalism and Social Policy in Australia, Canada, Great Britain and the United States*, Cambridge and New York: Cambridge University Press.

Obinger, Herbert, Stephan Leibfried and Francis G. Castles (eds) (2005), *Federalism and the Welfare State: New World and European Experiences*, Cambridge and New York: Cambridge University Press.

OECD (2011), *United We Stand: Why Inequality Keeps Rising*, Paris: OECD.

OECD (2015), *In It Together: Why Less Inequality Benefits Us All*, Paris: OECD.

Oliver, Rebecca and Margitta Mätzke (2014), 'Childcare expansion in conservative welfare states: policy legacies and the politics of decentralized implementation in Germany and Italy', *Social Politics*, **21** (2), 167–93.

Olivier, Cecilia and Brid Brennan (2010), 'Regional social policy from below: reclaiming regional integration—social movements and civil society organizing as key protagonists', in Bob Deacon (ed.), *World-regional Social Policy and Global Governance: New Research and Policy Agendas in Africa, Asia, Europe and Latin America*, London: Routledge, pp. 63–81.

Orenstein, Mitchell (2005), 'The new pension reform as global social policy', *Global Social Policy*, **5** (2), 175–202.

Orenstein, Mitchell (2008), *Privatizing Pensions: The Transnational Campaign for Social Security Reform*, Princeton, NJ: Princeton University Press.

Orloff, Ann Shola (1993a), 'Gender and the social rights of citizenship: the comparative analysis of gender relations and welfare states', *American Sociological Review*, **58**, 303–28, available at https://www.jstor.org/stable/2095903?seq=1#page_scan_tab_contents (accessed July 2016).

Orloff, Ann Shola (1993b), *The Politics of Pensions: A Comparative Analysis of Britain, Canada, and United States, 1880–1940*, Madison, WI: University of Wisconsin Press.

Orloff, Ann (2006), 'From maternalism to "employment for all": state policies to promote women's employment across the affluent democracies', in Jonah D. Levy (ed.), *The State After Statism: New State Activities in the Age of Liberalization*, Cambridge, MA: Harvard University Press, pp. 230–70.

Orloff, Ann (2009), 'Gendering the comparative analysis of welfare states: an unfinished agenda', *Sociological Theory*, **27** (3), 317–43.

Padamsee, Tasleem (2009), 'Culture in connection: re-contextualizing ideational processes in the analysis of policy development', *Social Politics*, **16** (4), 413–45.

Palier, Bruno (2005), 'Ambiguous agreements, cumulative change: French social policy in the 1990s', in Wolfgang Streeck and Kathleen Thelen (eds), *Beyond Continuity. Institutional Change in Advanced Political Economies*, Oxford and New York: Oxford University Press, pp. 127–44.

Palier, Bruno and Claude Martin (eds) (2008), *Reforming Bismarckian Welfare Systems*, London: Wiley-Blackwell.

Parreñas, Rhacel (2000), 'Migrant Filipina domestic workers and the international division of reproductive labor', *Gender and Society*, **14** (4), 566–80.

Parsons, Craig (2007), *How to Map Arguments in Political Science*, Oxford and New York: Oxford University Press.

Pascall, Gillian and Nick Manning (2000), 'Gender and social policy: comparing welfare states in Central and Eastern Europe and the former Soviet Union', *Journal of European Social Policy*, **10** (3), 240–66.

Paugam, Serge (ed.) (2011), *Repenser la solidarité: l'apport des sciences sociales*, Paris: Presses Universitaires de France.

Peck, Jamie and Nik Theodore (2010), 'Recombinant workfare, across the Americas: transnationalizing "fast" social policy', *GeoForum*, **41**, 195–208.

Peck, Jamie and Nik Theodore (2015), *Fast Policy: Experimental Statecraft at the Thresholds of Neoliberalism*, Minneapolis, MN: University of Minnesota Press.

Peng, Ito (2011), 'Social investment policy in South Korea', in Rianne Mahon and Fiona Robinson (eds), *Feminist Ethics and Social Policy: Towards a New Global Political Economy of Care*, Vancouver: UBC Press, pp. 94–110.

Peng, Ito (2012), 'The social and political economy of care in Japan and South Korea', *International Journal of Sociology and Social Policy*, **32** (11/12), 636–49.

Peng, Ito and Joseph Wong (2008), 'Institutions and institutional purpose: continuities and change in East Asian social policy', *Politics and Society*, **36** (1), 61–88.

Peoples Agenda for Alternative Regionalisms (n.d.), 'About PAAR', available at http://www.alternative-regionalisms.org/?page_id=2 (accessed 25 January 2016).

Pfau-Effinger, Birgit (2005), 'Culture and welfare state policies: reflections on a complex interrelation', *Journal of Social Policy*, **34** (1), 3–20.

Piketty, Thomas (2014) *Capitalism in the Twenty-first Century*, Boston, MA: Belknap Press of Harvard University Press.

Pierson, Paul (1993), 'When effect becomes cause: policy feedback and political change', *World Politics*, **45** (4), 595–628.

Pierson, Paul (1994), *Dismantling the Welfare State? Reagan, Thatcher, and the Politics of Retrenchment*, Cambridge and New York: Cambridge University Press.

Pierson, Paul (1996), 'The new politics of the welfare state', *World Politics*, **48**, 143–79.

Pierson, Paul (1998), 'Irresistible forces, immovable objects: post-industrial welfare states confront permanent austerity', *Journal of European Public Policy*, **5** (4), 539–60.

Pierson, Paul. (2011), 'The welfare state over the very long run', ZES Working Paper 02/2011.

Pleyers, Geoffrey (2011), *After Globalization/Global Justice: Becoming Actors in the Global Age*, Bristol: Polity.

Polanyi, Karl (1944), reprinted in 2001, *The Great Transformation: The Political and Economic Origins of Our Time*, Boston, MA: Beacon Press.

Powell, Martin and Ki-tae Kim (2014), 'The "chameleon" Korean welfare regime', *Social Policy and Administration*, **48** (6), 626–46.

Pribble, Jennifer (2011), 'Worlds apart: social policy regimes in Latin America', *Studies in Comparative Development*, **46**, 191–216.

Pribble, Jennifer (2013), *Welfare and Party Politics in Latin America*, Cambridge and New York: Cambridge University Press.

Quadagno, Jill (1984), 'Welfare capitalism and the Social Security Act of 1935', *American Sociological Review*, **45**, 632–47.

Quadagno, Jill (1988), *The Transformation of Old Age Security: Class and Politics in the American Welfare State*, Chicago, IL: University of Chicago Press.

Quadagno, Jill (1994), *The Color of Welfare*, Oxford and New York: Oxford University Press.

Radin, Margaret Jane (1996), *Contested Commodities*, Cambridge, MA: Harvard University Press.

Raghuram, Parvati (2012), 'Global care, local configurations—challenges to conceptualizations of care', *Global Networks*, **12** (2), 155–74.

Ray, Rebecca, Janet Gornick and John Schmitt (2010), 'Who cares? Assessing generosity and gender equality in parental leave designs in twenty one countries', *Journal of European Social Policy*, **20** (3), 196–216.

Rice, James J. and Michael J. Prince (2013), *Changing Politics of Canadian Social Policy* (second edn), Toronto: University of Toronto Press.

Rimlinger, Gaston (1971), *Welfare Policy and Industrialization in America, Germany and Russia*, New York: Wiley.

Rochefort, David A. and Roger W. Cobb (eds) (1994), *The Politics of Problem Definition: Shaping the Policy Agenda*, Lawrence, KS: University Press of Kansas.

Rojas, Cristina (2002), *Civilization and Violence: Regimes of Representation in Nineteenth Century Colombia*, Minneapolis, MN: University of Minnesota Press.

Rostgaard, Tine and Marta Szebehely (2012), 'Changing policies, changing patterns of care: Danish and Swedish home care at the crossroads', *European Journal of Ageing*, **9** (2), 101–9.

Sainsbury, Diane (1996), *Gender, Equality, and Welfare States*, Cambridge and New York: Cambridge University Press.

Sainsbury, Diane (2006), 'Immigrants' social rights in comparative perspective: welfare regimes, forms of immigration and immigration policy regimes', *Journal of European Social Policy*, **16** (3), 229–44.

Sainsbury, Diane (2012), *Welfare States and Immigrant Rights: The Politics of Inclusion and Exclusion*, Oxford and New York: Oxford University Press.

Saraceno, Chiara and Wolfgang Keck (2010), 'Can we identify intergenerational policy regimes in Europe?', *European Societies*, **12** (5), 675–96.

Sarvasy, Wendy and Patrizia Longo (2004), 'The globalization of care: Kant's world citizenship and Filipina migrant domestic workers', *International Feminist Journal of Politics*, **6** (3), 392–415.

Saunders, Diane (2015), 'Trump's true believers: how he's gone farther than Europe's far right, and who got him there', *Globe and Mail*, 13 December, available at http://www.theglobeandmail.com/news/world/how-trump-has-gone-farther-than-europes-far-right-and-who-got-himthere/article27713704/ (accessed 1 July 2016).

Schain, Martin (2008), *The Politics of Immigration in France, Britain, and the United States: A Comparative Study*, Basingstoke: Palgrave Macmillan.

Schmidt, Vivien A. (2002), 'Does discourse matter in the politics of welfare state adjustment?', *Comparative Political Studies*, **35** (2), 168–93.

Schmidt, Vivien A. (2011), 'Reconciling ideas and institutions through discursive institutionalism', in Daniel Béland and Robert H. Cox (eds), *Ideas and Politics in Social Science Research*, Oxford and New York: Oxford University Press, pp. 47–64.

Schön, Donald A. and Martin Rein (1994), *Frame Reflection: Toward the Resolution of Intractable Policy Controversies*, New York: Basic Books.

Sheahen, Allan (2012), *Basic Income Guarantee: Your Right to Economic Security*, Basingstoke: Palgrave Macmillan.

Shewell, Hugh (2004), *Enough to Keep Them Alive: Indian Welfare in Canada 1873–1965*, Toronto: University of Toronto Press.

Siaroff, Alan (1994), 'Work, welfare and gender equality: a new typology', in Diane Sainsbury (ed.), *Gendering Welfare States*, London: Sage, pp. 82–100.

Siim, Biirte and Anette Borchorst (2008), 'The multicultural challenge to the Danish welfare state—social politics, equality and regulating families', Feminist Research Centre in Aalborg, Paper 65, available via Research Gate, August 2015.

Silver, Hilary (1994), 'Social exclusion and social solidarity: three paradigms', *International Labour Review*, **133** (5–6), 531–78.

Silver, Hilary (2015), *Social Exclusion*, Cambridge: Polity.

Silver, Hilary and S.M. Miller (2003), 'Social exclusion: the European approach to social disadvantage', *Indicators*, **2** (2), 1–17.

Skocpol, Theda (1985), 'Bringing the state back in: strategies of analysis in current research', in Peter B. Evans, Dietrich Rueschemeyer and Theda Skocpol (eds), *Bringing the State Back In*, Cambridge and New York: Cambridge University Press, pp. 3–38.

Skocpol, Theda (1992), *Protecting Soldiers and Mothers: The Political Origins of Social Policy in the United States*, Cambridge, MA: Belknap Press of Harvard University Press.

Smith, Adam (1776), reprinted in 1991, *The Wealth of Nations*, New York: Random House.

Somers, Margaret and Fred Block (2005), 'From poverty to perversity: ideas, markets, and institutions over 200 years of welfare debate', *American Sociological Review*, **70** (2), 260–87.

Spiker, Paul (1991), 'The principle of subsidiarity and the social policy of the European Community', *Journal of European Social Policy*, **1** (1), 3–14.

Staab, Silke and Roberto Gerhard (2010), *Childcare Service Expansion in Chile and Mexico: For Women or Children or Both?*, Geneva: UNRISD.

Starke, Peter, Alexandra Kaasch and Frances Van Hooren (eds) (2013), *The Welfare State as Crisis Manager: Explaining the Diversity of Policy Responses to Economic Crisis*, New York: Palgrave Macmillan.

Steensland, Brian (2008), *The Failed Welfare Revolution: America's Struggle over Guaranteed Income Policy*, Princeton, NJ: Princeton University Press.

Steinmo, Sven, Kathleen Thelen and Franck Longstreth (eds) (1992), *Structuring Politics: Historical Institutionalism in Comparative Analysis*, Cambridge and New York: Cambridge University Press.

Stephens, John (1979), *The Transition from Capitalism to Socialism*, London: Macmillan.

Stone, Deborah (1997), *Policy Paradox: The Art of Political Decision Making*, New York: W.W. Norton.

Streeck, Wolfgang and Kathleen Thelen (eds) (2005a), *Beyond Continuity: Institutional Change in Advanced Political Economies*, Oxford and New York: Oxford University Press.

Streeck, Wolfgang and Kathleen Thelen (2005b), 'Introduction: institutional change in advanced industrial economies', in Wolfgang Streeck and Kathleen Thelen (eds), *Beyond Continuity: Institutional Change in Advanced Political Economies*, Oxford and New York: Oxford University Press, pp. 1–39.

Sumarto, Sudarno, Asep Suryahadi and Sami Bazzi (2010), 'Indonesia's social protection during and after the crisis', in A. Barrientos and D. Hulme (eds), *Social Protection for the Poor and Poorest: Concepts, Policies and Politics*, New York: Palgrave Macmillan, pp. 121–45.

Swank, Dwayne (2002), *Global Capital, Political Institutions, and Policy Change*, Cambridge and New York: Cambridge University Press.

Swenson, Peter (1997), 'Arranged alliance: business interests in the New Deal', *Politics and Society*, **25** (March), 66–116.

Tag, Miriam (2013), 'The cultural construction of global social policy: theorizing formations and transformations', *Global Social Policy*, **13** (1), 24–44.

Taylor-Gooby, Peter (ed.) (2004), *New Risks, New Welfare: The Transformation of the European Welfare State*, Oxford and New York: Oxford University Press.

Thelen, Kathleen (2004), *How Institutions Evolve: The Political Economy of Skills in Germany, Britain, the United States, and Japan*, Cambridge and New York: Cambridge University Press.

Tilly, Charles (1985), 'War making and state making as organized crime', in Peter B. Evans, Dietrich Rueschemeyer and Theda Skocpol (eds), *Bringing the State Back In*, Cambridge and New York: Cambridge University Press, pp. 169–91.

Tilly, Charles (1998), 'Where do rights come from?', in Theda Skocpol (ed.), *Democracy, Revolution and History*, Ithaca, NY: Cornell University Press, pp. 55–72.

Titmuss, Richard M. (1958), reprinted in 1963, *Essays on 'The Welfare State'*, London: George Allen & Unwin.

Titmuss, Richard M. (1974), *Social Policy*, London: George Allen & Unwin.

Tomiak, Julie-Ann (2011), 'Indigenous self-determination, neoliberalization and the right to the city: rescaling Aboriginal governance in Ottawa and Winnipeg', PhD dissertation, Carleton University.

Transnational Institute (n.d.), *Initiative People's Agenda for Alternative Regionalisms (PAAR)*, available at https://www.tni.org/en/network/initiative-peoples-agenda-alternative-regionalisms-paar (accessed 10 January 2016).

Tsing, Anna Lauenhaupt (2005), *Friction: An Ethnography of Global Connection*, Princeton, NJ: Princeton University Press.

UN Department of Economic and Social Affairs (2015), *Title of Page*, available at https://sustainabledevelopment.un.org/?manu=1300 (accessed 2 January 2016).

van Berkel, Rik and Iver Hornemann Møller (2002), *Active Social Policies in the EU: Inclusion through Participation?*, Bristol: Policy Press.

van Cott, Donna Lee (2006), 'Multiculturalism vs neoliberalism in Latin America', in Keith Banting and Will Kymlicka (eds), *Multiculturalism and the Welfare State: Recognition and Redistribution in Contemporary Democracies*, Oxford and New York: Oxford University Press, pp. 272–96.

van der Waal, J., W. de Koster and W. van Oorschot (2013), 'Three worlds of welfare chauvinism? How welfare regimes affect support for distributing welfare to immigrants in Europe', *Journal of Comparative Policy Analysis: Research and Practice*, **15** (2), 164–81.

van Hooren, Franca (2012), 'Varieties of migrant care work: comparing patterns of migrant labour in social care', *Journal of European Social Policy*, **22** (2), 133–47.

van Kersbergen, Kees and Philip Manow (eds) (2009), *Religion, Class Coalitions, and Welfare States*, Cambridge: Cambridge University Press.

van Kersbergen, Kees, Barbara Vis and Anton Hemerijck (2014), 'The great recession and welfare state restructuring: is retrenchment the only game left in town?', *Social Policy and Administration*, **48** (7), 883–904.

van Oorschot, Wim (2007), 'Culture and social policy: a developing field of study', *International Journal of Social Welfare*, **16**, 129–39.

Vetterlein, Antje (2015), 'Understanding policy change as position-taking: the IMF and social policies in times of crisis', in S. McBride, R. Mahon and G. Boychuk (eds), *After '08: Social Policy and the Global Financial Crisis*, Vancouver: UBC Press, pp. 87–104.

von Gliszczynski, Moritz and Lutz Leisering (2016), 'Constructing new global models of social security: how international organizations defined the field of social cash transfers in the 2000s', *Journal of Social Policy*, **45** (2), 325–43.

Wade, Peter (2004), 'Ethnicity, multiculturalism and social policy in Latin America: Afro-Latin (and indigenous) populations', ERSC seminar series on Social Policy, Stability and Exclusion in Latin America, 27 February, ILAS, available via the author.

Walker-Bourne, Astrid, Mark Gorman and Michael Bünte (2011), 'HelpAge International as a global actor', in Lutz Leisering (ed.), *Die Alten Der Welt Neue Wege der Altersschierung im Globalen Norden und Süden*, Frankfurt: Campus Verlag, pp. 395–429.

Walters, William (2000), *Unemployment and Government: Genealogies of the Social*, Cambridge and New York: Cambridge University Press.

Weaver, R. Kent (1986), 'The politics of blame avoidance', *Journal of Public Policy*, 6 (4), 371–98.

Weaver, R. Kent (2010), 'Paths and forks or chutes and ladders: negative feedbacks and policy regime change', *Journal of Public Policy*, 30 (2), 137–62.

Weaver, R. Kent and Bert A. Rockman (eds) (1993), *Do Institutions Matter? Government Capabilities in the U.S. and Abroad*, Washington, DC: Brookings Institute.

Weyland, Kurt (2006), *Bounded Rationality and Policy Diffusion: Social Sector Reform in Latin America*, Princeton, NJ: Princeton University Press.

Whiteside, H. (2015), 'Austerity budgets and public sector retrenchment: crisis era policy making in Britain, Canada and Australia', in S. McBride, R. Mahon and G. Boychuk (eds), *After '08: Social Policy and the Global Financial Crisis*, Vancouver: UBC Press, pp. 254–71.

Wilensky, Harold L. (1975), *The Welfare State and Equality: Structural and Ideological Roots of Public Expenditures*, Berkeley, CA: University of California Press.

Wilensky, Harold and C.N. Lebeaux (1958), *Industrial Society and Social Welfare*, New York: Russell Sage.

Williams, Fiona (1995), 'Race/ethnicity, gender, and class in welfare states: a framework for comparative analysis', *Social Politics*, 2 (2), 127–60.

Williams, Fiona (2012), 'Converging variations in migrant care work in Europe', *Journal of European Social Policy*, 22 (4), 363–76.

Williamson, John B. and Daniel Béland (2015), 'The future of retirement security in comparative perspective', in Linda K. George and Kenneth F. Ferraro (eds), *Handbook of Aging and the Social Sciences* (8th edn), San Diego, CA: Elsevier, pp. 461–81.

Wincott, Daniel (2006), 'Paradoxes of new labour social policy: toward universal childcare in Europe's "most liberal" welfare regime?', *Social Politics*, 16 (2), 286–316.

Wincott, Daniel (2011), 'Ideas, policy change and the welfare state', in Daniel Béland and Robert H. Cox (eds), *Ideas and Politics in Social Science Research*, Oxford and New York: Oxford University Press, pp. 143–66.

Wodak, R., M. Khosravinik and B. Mral (eds) (2013), *Right-wing Populism in Europe: Politics and Discourse*, London: Bloomsbury Academic.

Wood, Geof and Ian Gough (2006), 'A comparative welfare regime approach to global social policy', *World Development*, 34 (10), 1696–712.

World Bank (1994), *Averting the Old Age Crisis: Policies to Protect the Old and Promote Growth*, Oxford: Oxford University Press.

World Bank (2013), *Inclusion Matters: The Foundation for Shared Prosperity*, Washington, DC: The World Bank.

Yeandle, Sue, Teppo Kröger and Bettina Cass (2012), 'Voice and choice for users and carers? Developments in patterns of care for older people in Australia, England and Finland', *Journal of European Social Policy*, 22 (4), 432–45.

Yeates, Nicola (2008), 'The idea of global social policy', in Nicola Yeates (ed.), *Understanding Global Social Policy*, Bristol: Policy Press, pp. 1–20.

Yeates, Nicola (2012), 'Global care chains: a state of the art review and future directions in care transnational research', *Global Networks*, 12 (2), 135–54.

Yeates, Nicola (2014), 'The socialization of regionalism and the regionalization of social policy: contexts, imperatives', in Alexandra Kaasch and Paul Stubbs (eds), *Transformations in Global and Regional Social Policies*, New York: Palgrave, pp. 17–43.

Yeates, Nicola and B. Deacon (2010), 'Globalization, regional integration and social policy', in B. Deacon (ed.), *World-regional Social Policy and Global Governance: New Research and Policy Agendas in Africa, Asia, Europe and Latin America*, London: Routledge, pp. 27–40.

Yu, Hao (2015), 'Universal health insurance coverage for 1.3 billion people: what accounts for China's success?', *Health Policy*, **119** (9), 1145–52.

Index

Titles in the **Elgar Advanced Introductions** series include:

International Political Economy
Benjamin J. Cohen

The Austrian School of Economics
Randall G. Holcombe

Cultural Economics
Ruth Towse

Law and Development
Michael J. Trebilcock and Mariana Mota Prado

International Humanitarian Law
Robert Kolb

International Tax Law
Reuven S. Avi-Yonah

Post Keynesian Economics
J.E. King

International Intellectual Property
Susy Frankel and Daniel J. Gervais

Public Management and Administration
Christopher Pollitt

Organised Crime
Leslie Holmes

Nationalism
Liah Greenfeld

Social Policy
Daniel Béland and Rianne Mahon

International Conflict and Security Law
Nigel D. White

Comparative Constitutional Law
Mark Tushnet

International Human Rights Law
Dinah L. Shelton

Entrepreneurship
Robert D. Hisrich

International Trade Law
Michael J. Trebilcock

Public Policy
B. Guy Peters

The Law of International Organizations
Jan Klabbers

International Environmental Law
Ellen Hey

International Sales Law
Clayton P. Gillette

Corporate Venturing
Robert D. Hisrich

Public Choice
Randall G. Holcombe

Printed by Printforce, United Kingdom